MY FIRST TIME

MY FIRST TIME

STORIES OF SEX AND SEXUALITY
FROM WOMEN LIKE YOU

EDITED BY JEN THORPE

modjaji books

Publication © Modjaji Books 2012
Text © Jen Thorpe 2012
First published in 2012 by Modjaji Books PTY Ltd
P O Box 385, Athlone, 7760, South Africa
modjaji.books@gmail.com
http://modjaji.book.co.za
www.modjajibooks.co.za

ISBN 978-1-920590-04-8

Cover design: Carla Kreuser
Book design: Natascha Mostert
Project editor and compiler: Jen Thorpe
Copy editor: Nella Freund

Printed and bound by Mega Digital, Cape Town
Set in Garamond

CONTENTS

Introduction

WOMEN'S STORIES ARE important.

As women, we are told how to feel, look and act every day by a variety of sources, and when we're not doing it the 'right' way, we blame ourselves rather than the outside world. Every woman is taught to be self-critical— to wonder why she's not someone better, thinner, taller, brighter, sportier, healthier, more generous, more driven. These thoughts often form a negative cycle where we look further and further inside ourselves for the source of the problem, until we end up with our hearts and heads in crisis.

One of the most valuable things we can do to get ourselves out of this deep hole of self-loathing is to spend time with a girlfriend who has been there and who can empathise. With friends, we can reveal our darkest secrets, discuss our hopes, fears and dreams, and this sharing of our experiences builds us up in a way that the best diet or the most money can never do.

The *My First Time* project arose out of this idea that women are each other's foundations. Sometimes, for some reason, we don't have a confidante to tell our story to and these are times where a woman can almost burst with the weight of her own story. I began to feel there was a need for a space where women could share, a place where they knew they were not alone, and that there was someone out there who could share the experience.

I decided to make that space online and it began with a simple email project. I contacted women who I thought might like to be involved, and they were asked to invite women that they thought might like to be involved, and so on. This snowballing process generated enough interest for just over eighty women to start writing stories. Themes were suggested and writing was submitted. The stories blew me away.

I realised that keeping these accounts to myself in the hope that one day they would get published was delaying the process of sharing. I wanted the support to start immediately, not some time in the distant future. A blog seemed like the easiest and most accessible option to achieve this.

So I started http://myfirsttimessa.com. By February 2012 there were over 200 incredible stories on a range of themes and topics. This project grew in popularity online and has had over 300, 000 views since 2010.

Online, the women who wrote their amazing stories will remain nameless to protect them. We all know that sometimes we write a story not for it to be known as ours, but because we need to get it out. It needs to exist outside of us so that we can encounter it and deal with its source.

At the start of this project, my hope was that one day we would have a book of stories that you could give to your sister, your mother or your girlfriend. She would learn about women's experiences and perhaps feel better by reading something she identified with or by reading a positive story that inspired her to get through a rough patch. Maybe you would share it with her because you needed her to know a story that was similar to yours. Maybe she gave it to you, because she needed you to know.

My First Time is that book.

We've chosen to focus on sex and sexuality because, unfortunately, what can be one women's best part of her life can be another's worst, and also because it's the part that's least spoken about. Many experiences of sex are shrouded in such secrecy that they can feel impossible to articulate.

Well, we've done it. We've told some secrets. We've said what we needed to say about sex and sexuality, and we've collected it all for you.

This project has done so much to confirm my belief that women are powerful, empathetic, compassionate and courageous. I hope that you draw courage from the stories, that they move you and that they help you to start difficult or scary conversations with yourself and others. By reading this book, you are already empowering the contributors by thanking them for sharing their stories.

Love,

Jen

August 2012
Jen Thorpe, Curator of Stories

My First Orgasm

Anonymous

THREE YEARS AND one partner after I lost my virginity, I had my first orgasm.

The first guy I slept with was selfish both in and out of bed; sex was average at best. Foreplay was minimal and his technique was—for a supposedly sexually experienced man—decidedly poor. Sex became more of a chore than a pleasure and, being inexperienced and unconfident, I thought the reason I wasn't feeling satisfied was my fault, because *my* bits weren't working properly.

My next bedroom partner was a different kettle of fish. He was not only equally concerned with my pleasure, but probably more so than his own. Endless foreplay, glorious technique. For two years with him, however, the big O was still a no-show. I was getting to the 'brink' every time, but never quite got *there*. Despite this, I was loving sex for the first time and couldn't get enough of it. Sex was fine without orgasm, I thought.

I did wonder why I couldn't come. For the first year of our relationship I was on anti-depressants and knew that they inhibited orgasm (just what you need when suffering from depression). But, even when I stopped taking them, I still wasn't getting off.

Then suddenly, one day, it happened. I stopped focusing on the fact that I wasn't coming, accepted that it might not happen and then—BOOM—it snuck up on me. When I let go of my inhibitions and my expectations, there it was, hiding behind them. And, man, was it worth the wait!

My husband asked me recently to explain what my orgasms felt like—I think he was a little in awe of how I reacted each time when I came: out of control, as loud and as jerky as Beyonce's dance technique (apparently this looks sexy, I'm not so sure).

This was my answer: it starts as a wild, pulsing heat down below and this heat quickly ripples through the rest of my body in massive shockwaves of pleasure. You could ask me my own name in that moment and I wouldn't know—my brain completely empties and I am wholly at the mercy of my body.

Compared to what I actually feel, that is a crappy, cheesy description, but it's the best I can come up with. It seemed to satisfy my husband's curiosity and stoke his envy…considering the average clitoris has twice the amount of nerve endings as the penis, and that they are concentrated into a much smaller space, the female orgasm has the potential to be that much more explosive (another reason to be happy to be female!).

I now regularly enjoy orgasms and even find I tend to get cranky if I haven't had one in a while. There is something so head-clearing and perspective-making about something so simple and yet pleasurable that you can share with the person you love. And multiple orgasms—what's not to love about them? From time to time I still 'chase' my orgasm away if I'm stressed or too hung up on getting there, but I know it's just around the corner and will pop back to say hi soon.

The First Time I Separated Love And Sex

Amanda Simpkins

SEX IS EVERYWHERE. Books. TV. Movies. Magazines. We're surrounded by it even before we fully become aware of what it is. It seems like our lives are meant to revolve around this act: anticipating it, pursuing it, engaging in it. After all, sex is tied up with the idea of the much sought-after Fairy Tale True Love. How many hours are spent contemplating meeting 'that someone' and what you would do with him if left alone in a room together? I wondered why didn't I want those things? Doesn't everyone?

I had a wonderful, if uneventful, childhood. My parents were conservative, but not overbearingly so. My mom would frown at the perpetual chaos of scattered toys, but say nothing. She allowed us to be children. When afternoons at the playground transitioned to weekends at the mall, she broached the topic of sex. My mom sat me down and gave me a book explaining the mechanics of sex. She counselled me to wait until marriage, and I had no problem with that. I was only twelve and boys were alien creatures as far as I was concerned.

By the time I entered high school, men and relationships had become a favourite topic of discussion among my friends. I didn't have much to contribute there. Occasionally I crushed on someone who I found handsome or intriguing, but for the most part I remained uninterested. By senior year, I still had never dated anyone but, since I was happy by myself, this didn't particularly disturb me.

In college, I had a great deal more exposure to the opposite sex. In bars, at frat parties, at Pictionary night and church socials, they made the moves, which I deflected with ninja-like skill. When I brushed off the inferior males, I told myself that I was just picky. I was waiting for THE one. He would be wonderful. Something would click and I would feel that 'burning passion' or the 'electric spark.' I would be drawn to him 'like the tide to the moon', like every overdrawn metaphor you've ever heard. I would *want* to give myself to him.

Except he never showed up. No one even tempted me. Other girls detailed their random hook-ups and make-out sessions, but I never understood their interest. I told myself I was just a bit prudish.

After I graduated, I took a hard look at myself. By 23, I had still never gone on a single date. I was still waiting for my first kiss. I began to get anxious. I was supposed to have accomplished these things much earlier. My friends were getting married and having babies already. I was so behind them, I felt almost freakish. What was wrong with me?

Then he showed up.

He was everything I could have ever asked for. I felt so comfortable with him that I lowered my defences and set nervousness aside. We shared similar experiences, and both had a love of mysteries, exploring, and baked goods. We both wanted a family and a house with a tower. Our favourite method of flirting was texting each other the most challenging riddles we could dig up. As he lived two hours away from me, we could only get together occasionally, but after every date, I headed home grinning like an idiot. I couldn't get him off my mind. This was serious.

While he was entirely respectful, and I never felt pressured, after a few dates I realized that we had come to the part of our relationship where we were supposed to be kissing (at least). I considered this in a detached, academic way. I had no objections, because I really liked him. A romantic relationship was supposed to progress from handholding to kissing and, ultimately, to sex.

On our next date, I could tell the mood had shifted—there was something insistent about the way he searched out my hand, the looks he cast my way. My stomach churned, more with discomfort than anticipation. *That's only natural*, I told myself. *This is my first everything.* I tried to believe it. When we said our good-byes, I knew this was it. He leaned in. I steeled myself and moved towards him.

It was not what I expected.

I felt nothing. Not a thing. Where was the passion, this spark I had heard so much about? He obviously did not share my lack of enthusiasm. His arms wrapped around me, he nuzzled my neck. I cast a glance over his shoulder at the clock, wondering how long I had to wait before I could politely excuse myself. I was miserable.

I tried not to cry the whole bus ride home. I really cared for this guy. Even though our relationship was new, I could see myself growing old with someone like him. He had made me so happy…until that night. Why, if I cared so much for him, had I not felt the slightest urge to kiss him? Why had I felt nothing when it happened? Instead of cementing our relationship, I felt like he'd driven a stake into it. I doubted myself, I doubted everything.

Back at my apartment, I took recourse to the internet. I wanted to know what was wrong with me. During my search, I found asexuality.org. I had never heard of an asexual before. It had never even occurred to me to question my sexuality. I mean, I knew I had options. I was acquainted with all the different letters in LGBT and, while I had never been boy-crazy, I certainly had never felt anything for girls.

I didn't know it was possible for a person not to be sexually attracted to anyone at all. In our sex-permeated culture, where a high libido seems the norm, and where love often equals sex, I struggled to fathom that many people do not ever feel the inclination for sex. They're not celibate, depriving themselves of pleasure. Instead, like myself, they are wired never to feel the urge. And it's normal.

A weight lifted and suddenly my whole life made a lot more sense. All the excuses I had presented for my lack of interest (a conservative upbringing, high standards, nervousness, being prudish) had kept me from examining the underlying cause. I tried to think of a single time I had felt the slightest inclination to do something sexual and came up with nothing.

Perhaps most importantly, for the first time I realized that there is a clear distinction between love and sex. While the latter may never appeal to me, the first is still absolutely a possibility.

He texted me the next day. Without hormones clouding his judgment, he'd started to question our goodbye. He said that in retrospect something felt off and asked me if he had 'done wrong by me'. He had had a hard time reading me, and he understood if I wanted to just be friends. I replied I was interested in a romantic relationship, but that I couldn't promise I would ever want to express myself physically in the way that he would like. I couldn't quite bring myself to use the A-word (it was still a fairly new concept), but I did ask him if the lack of a physical relationship was a deal-breaker.

He said it was not.

I'm not sure he'll always feel that way. As I understand it, most people have some need for sex. He desires me in a way I can never reciprocate, and one day, in spite of our best attempts to compromise, that realization may be too much for him. Was I selfish in that decisive moment by asking him to be more than a friend? For now, fueled with hope and a willingness to communicate, we're trying to make it work.

Amanda Simpkins likes vintage fashion and travel.

The First Time I Touched A Penis

Anonymous

WHEN I WAS 19 and in my first year of university, I took a bus to Grahamstown to visit a friend during the holidays. I remember sitting by the window at the Midrand station while the bus waited to pick up passengers. I looked out and there was one person who caught my eye. He was tall, slim, had blondish brown hair and startling blue eyes. I went back to my novel and, as the new passengers came on board, I continued to read. The bus started and, as we drove out of the station, I put my book down. When I looked up, I found the blue-eyed boy sitting across the aisle from me in the same row. We made eye contact, he smiled, I smiled back and got a tingly feeling in my tummy.

As the bus drove on to Joburg station, we got to chatting and we found we had so much in common. It was easy to talk to this guy, we discussed everything and anything. Nothing sounded strange or embarrassing; we were open and honest and laughed the whole way to Joburg. At Joburg station, many new passengers came on and the driver told us we had to sit in our assigned seats. I picked up my bag and made my way to my allocated seat a few rows back. Next thing I knew, Mr Blue Eyes was right behind me and I turned to ask, "Where are you sitting?" He showed me his ticket. "NO way," I said. His assigned seat was the one next to me. We were convinced this was Fate and shared a smile.

It seemed Fate wanted to have a bit more fun, because our bus was delayed for four hours and we had to get off the bus. The two of us sat outside and the hours literally flew past. By the time the bus was ready, it was dark. Many passengers hopped on and instantly fell asleep.

Neither of us fell asleep. Instead we began to kiss, slowly, and it was absolutely delicious. I remember feeling excited and thinking to myself, "What am I doing!" A blanket was covering us and, I'm not sure how we managed to do so, but my jeans inched down and his zipper became undone. His fingers were gentle at first and then, sensing how much I was enjoying it, he began to rub me quicker and eventually his fingers were inside me. I was on cloud nine. I suddenly realised, "Oh, I am supposed to touch him too."

I touched his penis lightly with my fingers. It was hard and yet had the softest skin I have ever felt. I knew what I was supposed to do from movies and magazines, so I gave it my best shot, so to speak. Whatever I was doing must have been working, because the kisses became more fervent; I could see he was trying not to make too much noise. He came, it was hot and sticky on my hand and, thankfully, Mr Blue Eyes had a tissue for me.

Even though I had just met him, the situation didn't feel sleazy. It was one of the most exhilarating moments of my life. We chatted the whole long drive to the Eastern Cape. His stop was before mine, he promised to keep in contact with a flurry of kisses and a tight hug.

A few hours later I received an sms from him. We stayed in touch for a few years after that — nothing serious, just friends who had shared a moment and a 'first time' for me on a Greyhound bus.

The writer still enjoys road trips and flirts with Fate.

My First Experience Of Sexual Assault

Notsorandomgirl

IT HAPPENED SHORTLY after my 12th birthday. He was a good family friend—I had met him when I was nine years old. The day he started sexually abusing me was pretty ordinary, he came to pick me up from school as he sometimes did with permission from my mother. We went to get milkshakes and when he said he'd like to take me for a drive to Rhodes Memorial, I was excited as I had never been there before.

He found a quiet spot to park and asked me if I had seen a penis before. I found his question odd and replied no. He said, "You're a pretty girl. When your breasts start to grow, boys will want to take advantage of you." He said he would make it his duty to make sure that didn't happen. As that stage, I was totally blank as to what the connection was between having seen a penis and boys taking advantage of me because of my breasts.

He then unzipped his pants, took out his penis and asked, "Do you want to touch it?" I shook my head, looked out the window and asked him to take me home. He 'kindly' mentioned that it wasn't a question but an order, and proceeded to remind me that we were stuck in the middle of nowhere and he could do worse to me if I wasn't co-operative. Startled by how aggressive his tone was, I looked at him and saw that he wasn't joking.

I unwillingly touched his penis, not sure where or how I should be touching it. He guided me to stroke the shaft and go down all the way to his balls. I had never been that disgusted in my entire life. What repelled me most was the sound of his breath and the fact that he wanted to stick his tongue in my mouth. He squirted pre-cum, took my head with one hand, guided it to his crotch and ordered me to take his penis into my mouth.

I nearly puked. I had never experienced fear, disgust and humiliation in such an intense combination before. Fear that he might kill me, fear that no one would believe me. I wished I were dead rather than live through that experience. When he was satisfied, he asked me to slip a finger in my pussy but I couldn't move. It was as if I was suddenly paralysed. All I could do was cry.

He put his penis back into his pants, and said, "Stop crying." He made it clear that I was under no terms to tell anyone about the incident. After he had dropped me at home, I couldn't eat or touch my books for the rest of the day. I bathed twice and washed my mouth numerous times, but I still felt dirty inside. I felt dirty about the secret I had to keep.

That day was the beginnings of 14 months of sexual abuse where I got introduced to oral sex. My biggest fear was that he would rape me when he started indicating that he wanted to be the first person to have sex with me.

Notsorandomgirl loves blowing bubbles and dancing.

The First Time I Discovered There Was Such A Thing As Sex

Sarah Britten

MY MOTHER GOT away with murder, she really did. No patting the sofa cushions and inviting me to sit down. No explaining how when a man and a woman love each other very much, Things Happen. No clarification on where babies came from; in our household, they just materialized out of thin air.

Just as I reached the age where my mother was going to have to begin the awkward preamble to That Talk, I saved her the trouble by finding a copy of *Everywoman* amidst her sweaters. Who knows what I was doing ferreting in my mother's cupboard in the first place—probably looking for a hidden stash of Smarties—but one day, when I was ten years old, I felt the firm rectangular contours of a book amidst the soft folded fabric and decided to take a look.

First published in 1971, *Everywoman* was subtitled *A Gynaecological Guide For Life,* and it was comprehensive. It was also illustrated. The line drawings of the developing foetus didn't interest me. What did catch my attention were the illustrations in the first chapter, the one that explained where babies came from. I knew instantly, thrillingly, that what I was seeing—a naked man and woman entangled in couplings of various descriptions—was forbidden. I savoured that chapter like ice cream and chocolate sauce, gazing at the pictures, pouring over the text. I was careful to hide it back where I had found it, and my mother never suspected a thing.

For weeks I consulted regularly with *Everywoman*. Being thorough, I cross-referenced the revelations contained within its pages with the 1983 edition of the *World Book Encyclopedia*. Sex, explained the entry in the top left hand corner of page 264 of volume 17, "…is what makes males and females different from each other. It also attracts them to each other and involves deep feelings and desires." Alas, there were no pictures, so I soon lost interest, turning instead to volume 15 for Penis, which should have been between Pemmican and Penmanship, but was disappointingly absent. Volume 20 was little better; vaginismus was listed—it sounded unpleasant—but not vagina. (I never heard the word pronounced, so—and this is the most embarrassing revelation in this entire essay—until I was at university I assumed it was pronounced *vay-geena*.)

I was unusually good at drawing for my age, and I sketched obsessively, mostly horses, ballerinas and fighter jets. Naturally I translated my newfound discoveries onto the pieces of scrap paper that served as my sketchpad. As I recall, the positions were variations of what I had seen in *Everywoman* and, since they were fairly athletic, required some skill to render.

The most reliable source of the nudity that now fascinated me was art. I paged through my mother's art books in search of inspiration. In one pencil drawing I still vividly recall, I adapted Titian's *Venus of Urbino* and introduced a male figure into it, assiduously performing cunnilingus on the reclining lady. God knows how I concocted this scenario, because it would be another three years before I became aware of the existence of fellatio, and another four years after that before it occurred to me that the reverse was possible. (I learned about gay sex during a Plett holiday after I finished writing Matric, thanks to an enlightening discussion about AIDS between an aunt and a cousin.)

It was easy to be innocent then. I grew up in a household which in many ways was painfully prudish and, being the eldest, there were no older and more experienced siblings to cast the scales from my innocent eyes. My father might have taught us all the word 'scatophagy' because he thought it was funny, but the possibility that there might be something so bizarrely mechanical, yet utterly fascinating, as sex simply did not exist.

Everywoman changed all of that. Having established the existence of this marvelous, forbidden thing called sex, I searched high and low for descriptions of it. It wasn't easy; my grandmother's copies of *Cosmopolitan* were the most reliable sources, especially when they contained extracts from the latest Shirley Conran book.

By the time I was 12 and in Standard 5, I thought I knew almost everything there was to know. When we were divided into boys and girls and trooped into the hall to watch a flickering documentary on how babies were made, I cringed. Many of my classmates were genuinely enthralled because this was all new to them, but I felt embarrassed by their wide-eyed ignorance. Much as my mother would have felt, I think, knowing that I was reading *Everywoman*.

I was less careful about hiding my drawings than I was about replacing the book, and one awful day my mother discovered them. (Not the *Venus of Urbino*; that would have been unbearable.) She was horrified, as I knew she would be. Shame bloomed up my neck and into my cheeks as she admonished me. She threw the drawings away, and I returned to horses, ballerinas and fighter jets, but I could not banish what I had learned from my mind. The discovery of the drawings of sex in *Everywoman* inevitably led to fantasies about it, and they have been a source of pleasure and comfort ever since.

Seven boyfriends and one divorce later, my mother and I have yet to have a conversation about sex. She knows what I get up to, and she has an opinion on it, but she cannot bring herself to utter the 'S' word, and I cannot bring myself to say it to her. Watching the lesbian scene with her in Black Swan was agony beyond the power of words to describe.

Sex happens, but there's no need to talk about it, and never was. Not when there are books hidden amongst

the sweaters in a cupboard, filled with marvelous things
waiting to be revealed.

*Writer, blogger and artist, Sarah Britten was born in Johannesburg
in 1974 and studied Drama at Wits University. She has worked
for more than 10 years as a strategist in the advertising industry.
Her interest in advertising led her to write her PhD thesis on the
contribution of the former to national identity in post-apartheid
South Africa. She has published five books, including three
collections of South African insults.*

The First Time I Was The Other Woman

Anonymous

WOMEN TALK ABOUT how men cheat, the bastards! Our cheating, we don't talk about as much. Or, if we do, we usually try to rectify or moralise the affairs. I mean, after all, who wants to be a slore (as those silly Kadashians put it)?

So we disguise our devious deeds as romance: "I wasn't just the other woman, we're in love." Or, "I was overwhelmed by his persistence and powers of seduction." Or, "I tried, but he just never took no for an answer." What self-delusion and half-truths!

When I tumbled into bed with the dude who didn't belong to me, I found that my whole mind was in a haze. Morality dissolved, I couldn't think straight. I'm not surprised, sexual attraction is a kind of drug, isn't it? I'd seen his partner plenty of times and I knew he was really in love with her. When I saw her, I felt a strange coolness, a surreal detachment as I processed the lies it must have taken for her man to get to me. Then, the feeling would pass. She was a lovely, strong woman and I knew I was a passing, flitting thing.

The first time it happened, it was such a rush, such a thrill. I was surprised by the lengths he would go to to see me. Maybe it was because he wasn't afraid of taking the risk. That's why men get caught so easily, they'll tell the dumbest lies when they're late. As a woman, I would be more cautious and strategic. When I asked him about guilt, he was obviously free of it. The reason was that we weren't in love. We didn't really want to know much about each other and yet the sex was delicate, loving and really awesome.

That was the problem right there; I realised a meaningful sexual connection could develop between two people where morals and love were absent. I hadn't known this before. It scrambled the moral circuit of my upbringing that said, "Women only want sex with love," and "The only good sex is married sex," or "Women are more emotional; one-night stands can hurt you." All that fell away and, to be honest, I just breathed. I realised this was me, right now, and felt a wave of confidence about myself I had never felt before.

But taking someone else's someone is a messy business–it's better ended soon, lest you do end up being attached. So I have struggled to write this, because I don't feel guilty about what I did, yet it feels like I should say I feel bad. I know if you've been cheated on, you must have hated that other person, who must have seemed selfish or desperate.

Desperate? I wasn't desperate, just in need of having that person for a moment and then moving on. I don't want to seem as if I am justifying or glamorising my actions. I'm just saying—the first time I had sex with someone else's man, I didn't feel guilty and it was some of the best sex ever.

My First Pregnancy Announcement

Nicolettus-Stiffneckus

AT 17, IN my last year of school, I had never held hands with a boy, kissed a boy, or even thought of boys in any other way than 'a friend who was not a girl'. I'd always been tall for my age and with it came the assumption that I was more mature than my friends. The truth was that I was almost more than innocent: my ignorance bordered on not even knowing the acceptable roles for men and women.

So when my tummy started to get bigger, the last thing on my mother's mind was pregnancy. I thought it was a gross case of constipation. My mother and I went to the doctor together. When he saw my firm tummy pushing against my clothing, he pronounced the happy occasion with mirth, "Your daughter is pregnant!" (Note no examination was deemed necessary.)

I recall my mother turning to me and asking "Are you pregnant?" Just those three words and a look that could turn the sun into a wasted star. I said, "No!", shocked that she could even think that. The doctor ignored me, and said quietly to my mother, "They always deny it, sometimes right up until the birth." My mother, of whom I am sometimes afraid, slowly turned to me and said nothing, but her eyes said, 'You had better prove him wrong'.

I was reeling with shock and lost in a capsule of confusion. I had just recently discovered that I could bring myself pleasure by touching my body. I hadn't even found the right word to name it yet. Could this be the result—a baby? Burning with embarrassment, I asked the doctor, "Is there any way of getting pregnant other than by sleeping with a boy?"

My mother quickly interjected before the doctor could answer my question. "She is definitely not pregnant." This statement brought the doctor round to admitting that there could be another reason other than unprotected adolescent sex. I stepped alone into the examination room, terrified, not knowing what to expect.

After the examination, he stuck to the initial diagnosis: "I can feel the foetus and hear the heartbeat." I felt horribly exposed and violated and I stuck to my story, "No, I am not pregnant." Blood was taken and the result came back inconclusive. What did that mean? By then I had become an interesting case for the doctor and a second test was done. It came back negative and I was whisked off to a specialist.

What the doctor had heard was not a heartbeat, nor had he felt a foetus; it was, in fact, an ovarian cyst pulsating rhythmically.

Since then I have only trusted female doctors; their bedside manners are so much more refined.

Nicolettus-Stiffneckus (her blog name) enjoys a hearty laugh and is preparing for a zombie invasion.

The First Time I
Knew I Was Raped
Michelle Solomon

THE FIRST TIME I realised it was actually rape was the day after it happened. I didn't want to think about it. It was easy to ignore what had happened, because we didn't live in the same town. But now I have to face him. I'm moving back there, to where he lives. And I'm terrified.

I knew it was rape, but I wouldn't believe that it was. Not until I started reading the columns and news stories during the 16 Days of Activism against Women and Child Abuse. That's when I knew it was rape.

While denying what had happened to me, I participated in all the protests in the 1-in-9 campaign. I taped my mouth shut for 24 hours in solidarity with the eight out of nine rape survivors who, because of social pressure, never report their rapes. I fought for the rights of rape survivors, I prayed for them, and voiced my anger at the denial of their justice. I cried with them and laughed with them.

Now, three years later, and here I sit denying myself my own justice. Because I am too shit scared.

He was a friend of mine, my ex-boyfriend's best friend. He was my closest friend's ex-boyfriend. He was a serial womaniser who treated women as the means to satiate his sexual desires. I once heard he had slept with over 70 women. I am now one of them. How many others also said, "No"?

We were friends and I tried to support him through his break-up with my close friend. But, because I have breasts and a vagina, he saw my support as sexual flattery. I told him then, months ago, sex between us would never happen. It was too complicated; too many people would get hurt. "It will never happen," I told him.

How naïve.

He told me he wanted to do 'naughty things' to me, but if I didn't want it, he would 'control' himself. Even when I told him the sexual jokes and comments he said made me uncomfortable, he continued with them.

So I avoided him. I wouldn't go to see my friends in the town where he lived because I was scared I would see him. He asked me why I wouldn't visit. In jest, I told him it was because I didn't trust him.

"You can trust me," he said, "but not when I've been drinking, ha ha."

I told him again and again it would never happen between us. He said he understood. He said, "You're still my super journo friend whom I respect whole heartedly (sic)." I believed him.

How stupid. How absolutely incredibly fucking stupid.

He came to my town; I suggested we meet up for drinks for old time's sake. I was lonely, vulnerable in a new town, and wanted a friend to hang out with at a bar. Afterwards he came to my house, so I could introduce him to my dogs. I love my dogs—they mean everything to me. I was black-out drunk when we got home. I don't remember much.

I do remember he kissed me. I do remember he carried me to my bedroom. I do remember he undressed me.

And I do remember saying no. I do remember stopping him. I do remember telling him that too many people would get hurt if we did this. I remember telling him I cared too much about my friend. I don't remember what he said in response, and I don't remember what I said then.

But I know he didn't stop.

The next day my thighs and my vagina hurt. I lay on my couch all day thinking about what happened. I showered twice, cried and hugged my dogs. I slept on the couch that night, because I didn't want to go near my bed—the scene of the crime.

I considered laying a charge at the police. I have written evidence that I had told him, months prior to that night, that I didn't want to have sex with him. But would they believe me? I was drunk, he was at my house where I live alone with my two dogs. I took him home the next day. He had a reputation for sleeping around. Would anyone believe that I had said, "No"? That I tried to stop him? That I physically covered my vagina with my hands and told him, in no uncertain terms, I did not want to have sex with him?

No one knows about that night. If I laid a charge against him, my friend will know. I don't want to hurt her.

Everyone will know about that night and they'll make my life hell by saying it wasn't rape. They'll question why I only reported it now, months after the fact. They will question, question, question.

Now I am moving back to the town where he lives. It's a small town, and we have the same friends. What the fuck am I supposed to do? I feel like I am betraying the cause by not charging him with rape.

But, God, I am so scared. What should I do?

Michelle is an anti-rape activist in her home town. When not doing rape awareness and education with young men and women, she is a media studies student and academic. She works with other rape survivors against rape and gender-based violence. In solidarity.

My First HIV Test

Sarah Haken

I'M A RELATIVELY responsible person. I don't drink and drive, I pay all my bills on time, people can rely on me. Why then was I happy to have sex without a condom? Oh, I thought I was being 'responsible'—he was my long-term boyfriend and I figured he would be HIV negative. Did I ask him? No. It didn't even cross my mind until a couple of weeks later.

I was going out that evening, and he was staying in. When I went to say goodbye, he said, "I have something to tell you." He told me he had had an HIV/AIDS test. I didn't say anything, I just looked at him. He asked, "Well, aren't you going to ask me the result?" I can't remember what I answered, I suppose, "Yes". I just remember thinking, "You bastard. You sick, mean asshole. You put me at risk when you yourself never knew." Perhaps this was the beginning of the end of our relationship? I can›t be sure. He told me, "Negative".

I breathed a sigh of relief and went out with my friends. I got horrendously drunk. Then I remembered there was a three-month window period. My boyfriend had been with a number of 'questionable' girls prior to myself. And hey, if he didn't feel the need to use a condom with me, why would it have been any different with them? *Stupid, stupid me.* I decided that I should wait and go and get tested myself after three months.

Those three months came and went, they turned into six months, then 12, then two years, and then three... and now almost four years. I think I told only three people during that period about my fear, and two only very recently.

During that time, my boyfriend and I ended. We move in different worlds now, we barely even talk anymore. I have not been with anyone since.

But I was thinking about him today, thinking about what I would say to him if I was HIV positive, because I finally went for the test.

I was negative.

Such relief. I wanted to cry for that naïve, girl who gave herself to someone who abused her trust, cry for that girl who knew how to do everything correctly, but didn't. I wanted to cry for that girl who had spent years agonising over going for a simple test, and, when finding out, felt like a weight had been lifted. I wanted to cry, but instead, I smiled.

Finally, I knew my status. Do you know yours?

Sarah Haken is a lawyer in Johannesburg.

My First Time Was Natural

Jen Thorpe

IN MANY NON-VERBAL ways, we'd been planning it for a few days. Despite us both being virgins, and despite us only having dated for a few months, the idea came naturally. One night we went up to his room after a few glasses of Dutch-courage, and began kissing.

It's funny, because in the movies it always seems awkward, uncomfortable, with a lot of umming and aahing about where things fit, asking if you're ready, and lots of pauses to gaze into each other's eyes in affirmation.

For us, there was no awkwardness. The music was cheesy, but memorable. The lights were dim, but bright enough to see. There were no pauses. We didn't need verbal affirmation. There was so much love. The whole thing flowed as if it had always been happening.

The next day I couldn't stop smiling. The best thing was that when I saw him later that day, he couldn't stop smiling either.

Jen Thorpe is a feminist writer and researcher who is still in love with her first time.

The First Time
I Experienced
Sexual Harassment

Damaria Senne

THE YEAR WAS 1985. I had just turned 17, I was at university and living away from home for the first time. Having been raised by over-protective parents, I hadn't ever been anywhere or done anything without a family member present. Moving away from Phokeng in the North West Province to Fort Hare University in the Eastern Cape was a challenge for me.

I wasn't assimilating well into university life. The culture was different and the academic demands onerous. Regular student strikes resulted in a strong police presence, which made me feel even less secure in the environment. I was getting increasingly worried that these challenges would result in my failing, which would have been disastrous because my parents were paying for my studies. They needed me to graduate from university on schedule so they could focus on educating my younger brother. My parents couldn't afford to pay full university fees for both of us at the same time—I had to pass or fall by the wayside.

I was therefore relieved when one of my lecturers offered to tutor me privately. After I arrived at his office on time for our first appointment, we talked about why I was having problems with his subject and how he could help me. But then he stood up, walked around his desk and pulled me to my feet. I was stunned.

Did I mention that many 12 year olds I interact with today know more about the opposite sex and how to rebuff unwanted attention than I did at 17? My mind shut down when he pulled me into his arms, all I could think about was getting away. I struggled and shouted and pushed at him until he let me go.

The man spoke rudely to me, with a few words in isiXhosa which I didn't understand, but the tone was unmistakeable. As I grabbed my books and left, I realised the door had been open all along and people must have walked by. Sometimes I wonder how that incident would have ended if he had closed the door—would he have let me go when I struggled?

I'd love to say that my lecturer was embarrassed by the event and treated me with respect from then on, but that would not be true. The incident became a starting point for his campaign to undermine me and he chose to attack my work, where it hurt the most.

He didn't give me the opportunity to ask questions in class, even when I raised my hand to attract his attention. I missed chunks of information when he sometimes spoke in isiXhosa. He never indicated that the incident was in the past, so I couldn't relax and focus on my studies. I remained afraid of him and my studies faltered. I remained silent in shame, not telling my friends about the incident or explaining why I was suddenly persona non grata to that lecturer. Nor did I report the incident to authorities, though thinking back, I realise there was a lecturer who would have helped me if he had known.

What I did do was study harder and work more closely with my classmate friends so they could ask the questions in class I couldn't. With relief, I passed at the end of the year and took the opportunity to transfer to another university. A less-known and less-respected university, but I was thrilled to continue studying in a less hostile environment.

Later I learnt that the lecturer regularly had affairs with female students, yet many people condemned the students' actions and said nothing about the lecturer. As an adult now, I realise that those female students must have felt they had little choice in the matter. If others sugar-coated these students' harassment and abuse and chose to call it an affair, what could the students do?

I also discovered that the lecturer had daughters. I wonder how he would have reacted if he learnt that the people teaching his children were acting as reprehensibly as he had. Would he have seen wrong in his actions, if it had hit closer to home?

Damaria Senne is a writer and publisher who loves tech toys, gardening and renovating old houses.

My First Time Breastfeeding

Jacqueline Setti Hardman

I THINK ONE of the gross things about being a woman is breastfeeding. I mean, almost every woman who has a child has to go through it, but that still didn't make it okay for me.

My daughter's first suck on my over-sized, melon breasts came as such a relief. My boobs were hard, huge and screaming for someone to suck on them. Out of the context of sex, that urge could have been disturbing, but was normal under those circumstances.

My husband was not a breast man, thankfully, and I got away with that nipple-sucking thing most men do to their women. So I was horrified when I discovered I was having a baby boy. I'd heard all sorts of stories about how baby boys get excited when they feed. Gross, right? What mother wants to feed her boy child if things happen to him physically while on the breast?

Thankfully, my son didn't breastfeed for long, which I feel responsible for because I think he could sense I was uncomfortable with it. He must have felt the vibes, but try as I might, I couldn't get those horrible images out of my head. He stopped breastfeeding when he was nine months old, compared to my daughter who breastfed for two years. To be honest, I didn't feel weird about her breastfeeding because she was a girl.

With breastfeeding, there also comes pain. The worst pain I have experienced was blocked ducts and the awful part is that the child still needs to feed even when you have a blocked duct.

The weird thing about breastfeeding, though, is that when I stopped doing it, I wished to do it again. It became addictive. I started coaxing my toddlers to come lie on my chest so I could feel that connection again. But being toddlers, they didn't do it.

But for all that, when I breastfed for the first time, I knew that I had entered motherhood. For me, it was the ultimate rite of passage.

Jacqueline Setti Hardman is a mother of three with a passion for life.

The First Time Someone Touched My Vagina

Athambile Masola

THERE ARE ONLY a few words available in isiXhosa to refer to a vagina in a pleasant way—*usisi, inhenhenhe, ikuku, umphantsi*. When I was young, I viewed mine as being merely functional insofar as my menstrual cycle and other biological functions were concerned. I was happy with that.

Until a boy's curious hands to help me understand what my vagina is really about.

In Grade 9, our Bible Education teacher at school went through the implications of exploring sexuality with boys. The hidden message was that males were physical and females emotional. Because we, as girls, responded to sex emotionally, we should never let boys take advantage of us. Enjoying what happened between a boy and a girl was simply not an option—it would lead to the girl being called 'loose'.

In my early teens I had a chronic case of what my friends and I called 'the disease to please'. The main symptom of this illness was that if any boy showed an interest in me and made advances, he was bound to get the answer he was looking for. At primary school I had been described as playing hard to get and now I was loose. I can't explain how this radical shift happened—perhaps it was partly curiosity and partly searching for attention.

I had heard about being fingered but didn't know any of the details, so when it happened, I was shocked and unprepared. I have to say it was a pleasant surprise. I don't remember if the boy was my 'official boyfriend' or not, but whenever we went out we ended up kissing. The step from kissing to touching was not communicated, it just happened. His hands managed to find their way to my vagina while we were kissing and I remember sitting in a position that made it easy for him to venture 'down there'.

Later he started to kiss my vagina, an even more pleasant surprise. I had never realised my vagina had the possibility of evoking a good feeling. And that's how I became acquainted with the silence around sexuality: that it is not, in fact, dirty but something that can be enjoyable.

Yet a girl who let boys touch her was considered a bad girl and I didn't want to be bad for the rest of my teenage years. I soon learned to restrain myself, mostly by avoiding boys I found attractive lest they should venture 'down there' and release a flood of forbidden sensations and emotions. This attitude has carried over to my adult life and is taking a lot of work to undo, because the reality is that I am a woman with desires that I shouldn't be afraid of.

Athambile Masola is a feminist (high school) teacher.

My First Time In A War Zone

Robyn Kriel

"I SMELLED YOU from across the camp the moment you got out of the vehicle."

I resisted the urge to ask the handsome young United States Marine, who was helping me put on my 15-pound Kevlar bulletproof vest, whether it was a good smell or a bad smell. I was on day eight of no shower or bath, and figured I should spare myself the pain of the truth.

I was the only woman in a United States Marines Combat Outpost in Helmand Province, Afghanistan. I was surrounded by more than a hundred muscle-bound American males who hadn't seen a woman (or at least one not covered up from head to toe in a traditional Afghan burka) in six months. And I was on the verge of losing my mind.

"The shitters are over there."

I stared in horror at another young man who was pointing out, well, the shitters.

They were tented off 'areas' the size of telephone booths, containing a wooden box toilet seat and lid, one that was bedazzled with the name "WARLORD THRONE" on it. The tents had holes in them and nothing at the bottom, which meant everyone knew exactly who was in there and what they were doing, the entire time.

"Um, thanks," I mumbled. He then took me to a pile of 'Wag Bags' and began to explain what they were used for when I politely cut him off, and pointed out the bags came with directions. (A wag bag is a plastic bag the troops use when they go to the toilet.) I really didn't need someone younger than me telling me how to use the bathroom, although later that day I did still have to read the directions.

This was my life for the next month. Caked with sand, covered in sand flea bites, surrounded by men who were too shy even to look at me, never mind strike up a conversation, and trying to avoid getting my legs blown off by stepping on a humongous bomb.

War and journalism aside, I needed to talk to a woman. I was having problems that only another woman would understand. I am a girls' girl. I wanted to gossip, to laugh, and to talk about how much my boobs hurt under the Kevlar.

My boyfriend back home had picked a huge fight with me and told me I was being a diva, and I needed someone to tell me that I wasn't a diva, I was just experiencing battle fatigue, or something. My whole life I had been surrounded by a plethora of women. I had had a mother, a grandmother, a big sister and then hundreds of friends at my girls-only high school. In Afghanistan I learnt a lot about myself, and one thing I really need in my life is other women.

I needed to talk about the fact that cleansing down every night using baby wipes is not an acceptable way to live. I needed someone to ask if they were also horribly constipated from the barely edible, over-processed Meals Ready to Eat we had to eat. My cameraman and dear friend, Meshack Dube, was trying to look after me, and to be that person for me, but there are some things that even dear male friends just do not want or need to know.

I guess I could have gone to the (male and slightly cute) camp medic and begged for laxatives, but there was one other thing I knew that even a trained doctor, who could sew people's arms back on while bullets were flying around, could not help me with.

I was desperate, I mean to the point that I would have bribed, begged or stolen, for a tampon.

My doctor had advised me to skip my period while I went into battle, since there were no showers or really any basic necessities other than guns, ammunition and food. So I took the pill, followed her instructions, and it was all peachy until we got woken up in the middle of the night to go on a raid.

"Bring your flak jackets, your water bottles, sleeping bags and camera gear," said the six-foot-eight giant of a Gunnery Sergeant. "Don't bring any crap you don't need."

So I figured I would leave the baby wipes, extra underwear, deodorant, mirror to apply my make-up, moisturizer etc. What I forgot, though, was my box of birth control tablets. We were due to be gone for about 24 hours and we ended up being stuck in the middle of nowhere for close to three days. I smelled even worse than usual, and had gotten my period. I had no tampons and, well, no one to ask if I could borrow any and Helmand Province isn't the type of place you can go and pick some up at your local pharmacy.

I began to need to share my dilemma with someone. I considered emailing good friends, but I didn't have the heart or the strength to put my personal problems into words. It was blazing hot out there, desert heat, we were walking up to 20 kms per day with full gear and the fear of being gunned down. And I was cramping and miserable. Great. How am I supposed to tell some tough Marine that? I tried calling my Mom to tell her, but every time she heard that it was me over the satellite phone she started crying in relief that I was alive, and passed the phone to my Dad.

After one month, when I stumbled out of Combat Outpost Rankel and into the semi-civilized world of Forward Operating Base Deli, I saw the first woman I had seen in a month, and all bravado left me. I walked up to Sergeant Sanchez and said, fighting tears, "Hello. I'm Robyn and I'm a journalist. I need a tampon and my boyfriend is being really mean to me." She looked at me in a wizened way, and helped me out. And then she listened. That's what I really needed. Normality had returned.

I'm giving you the lowlights of my trip and, to be honest, they were few and far between. By the time I got back to South Africa, I was 5kgs lighter, my hair was green and falling out, and I was a different colour to when I left, but my life was changed forever. Both Meshack and I had been bitten by the battle bug. The troops we had covered were brave and gentlemanly, not once was anyone rude or mildly sexual towards me. They saved lives, both each others' and members of the local Afghan population. We had witnessed some of the most amazing scenes that will stay with me forever, and the harsh living conditions became completely and utterly worth it and addictive.

However, my first time in a warzone taught me two things: that I need to toughen my Mom up so we can talk on the phone next time, and as women our 'essential' items differ to those of men. No matter who is barking at you telling you to cut down your gear, always take with you a change of underwear, tampons, laxatives and more baby wipes than you think you could ever need. It might not save your life, but it will save your sanity.

Robyn Kriel is the East Africa Bureau Chief and senior correspondent for eNews Channel Africa, based in Nairobi, Kenya. She covers 11 countries including the always eventful South Sudan, Somalia and the Democratic Republic of Congo. Robyn was born and raised in Bulawayo, Zimbabwe. She has been blessed with a wonderful family and friends on several continents.

My First Time Using A Tampon

Anonymous

I BEGAN THE journey of change from girl to woman in a boarding house full of hormonal teenage girls. Together we experienced the same transformations in our bodies, minds and souls, we were becoming women. We shouted, fought, cried and hugged, usually in that order.

As we grew up, we sang and laughed together as we fell asleep under the same roof each night. We wrote long letters to each other, talked about boys in detail and wished for the day we would fall in love. Every detail of our womanhood was discussed and analysed as we tried to understand what was happening inside us.

In those days most girls including myself used sanitary pads, which were eventually deemed gross, messy and uncomfortable. I remember waking up in the middle of the night and having to change my sheets and my underwear, and sometimes even my pyjamas, because there was blood all over my bed. I was mortified by it, even though I was surrounded by other girls going through exactly the same experience.

I had a close bunch of friends at the time and one of them, the ballsiest and the leader of our small clan, suggested I start using tampons. I hadn't known about them before this. After becoming aware of my predicament, my friend was adamant that I was going to learn to use them.

So it was that one afternoon she pulled me along to our bathroom, with a pink tampon box in hand, to explain how they worked. She pulled out the instruction sheet and opened the page up to show me the picture. I remember feeling shy and embarrassed when I realised I would have to stick the thing up with my finger. I was scared it was going to hurt, that it would get stuck and never come out. I thought, "What if it gets stuck and someone else has to take it out?"

On the prompting of my friend, I finally took one out of the box and locked myself in one of the toilets with my friend standing by for encouragement. With a one quick movement, I pushed the tampon up into place and, feeling slightly uncomfortable, waddled out the bathroom.

I felt liberated and in charge the rest of the day, having faced the unknown and come out a woman. I have used tampons ever since and never looked back. Every now and then I remember that first time—I have a good chuckle at the whole experience and am reminded just how important it is to have girlfriends.

The writer is a primary school teacher who is happily engaged and believes in the power of love to overcome all obstacles.

My First Times: Kisses, Love and Loving Myself

Anonymous

My first kiss

If kissing-catchers in nursery school counts, then my first kiss was with V. That was disappointing, because I was madly in love with R who refused ever to kiss me after that.

My real first kiss was with a boy called G. It was a week after I had my braces removed, when I was fifteen years old. Again, disappointing. Ending up with slobber on my face was not what I had envisioned, or even received when practicing on my hand. Yuk, yuk, yuk.

The first time I fell in love

The first time I fell in love (real love, not the kind in primary school with L),was with my first serious boyfriend (M) when I was 18. I thought he was perfect for me.

The first time I told someone I loved him

The first time I told M that I loved him, he looked me in the eye like he was going to say it back, but instead told me that he had cheated on me the night before.

The first time someone told me they loved me

The first time someone told me that he loved me was during a fight about the fact that he had cheated on me. I suppose he thought that by saying it, I would miraculously forgive him.

The first time my heart was broken

The same night I told someone that I was in love with him.

The first time I loved who I was

I had a mini epiphany at the age of 22 and realised I love who I am. It's very sad that it is so late, but being cheated on constantly for three years will do that to a person.

The writer has since moved on, and is a happy-go-lucky person with a generally positive outlook on love and life.

My First Reactions To My Infertility

Kate Paterson

WHEN I STARTED chemotherapy for Hodgkin's lymphoma, I was told the chances of it affecting my fertility were slim. My doctor advised me against egg harvesting because she didn't feel comfortable delaying my chemo and because fertility treatment failed more often than it worked.

Unfortunately, the chemo didn't work the first time, so we set about preparing me for a stem cell transplant, which included two preliminary rounds of ICE chemotherapy. It was horrible stuff but the big one was still to come—a high dose chemo over six days that usually had long-term side-effects.

There would be enough time to harvest eggs before starting it, so I called the specialist, excited, as soon as I realised it was an option. My period was to start in three days' time and I had to be in hospital in five weeks' time to start chemo. The timing seemed perfect.

One of the first things the specialist asked when I called him was if I was married or in a committed relationship. Apparently the chances of any of my eggs becoming a live baby were infinitely higher if I could store a fertilised egg. My boyfriend had recently broken up with me, because life had dealt both of us blow after blow, but I knew that he still loved me and saw a future with me. I also knew that this was the only chance we could have a child together.

It was a strange conversation to have, to say the least, but he didn't even hesitate when I asked him to father my child. I think he was excited about it too— to have a little embryo tucked away somewhere could have been the first positive thing to happen in months. The specialist warned me not to get too excited—we still had to do tests to see if I was capable of harvesting—but I knew better. I knew that this was going to work because it had to work. It had to work like I had to live.

The doctor first had to check my hormone levels to see whether my ovaries had the potential to release eggs. I knew that, even if the levels were perfect, there was still a chance that my eggs would not be harvested, but I truly believed that hope and determination would get me through. I had been through a lot and I deserved this; God was going to give me a break. We sat in the waiting room for what seemed like forever, my ex-boyfriend and I filling out forms amongst the married couples and mothers-to-be. Feeling awkward and out of place, I wished I had someone that I could really share this problem with.

At two that afternoon we went back for the results. This time we were the only people in the waiting room and the doctor came straight out to welcome us. He was a tall, elderly man and was smiling from ear to ear. My heart was beating quickly, but just looking at him gave me a wave of relief and I knew that everything would be fine. I wouldn't have to worry anymore. We followed him into his room and sat down. His huge smile made me smile.

"It's not good news," he said.

It took a second for it to hit me and then I was crying uncontrollably. My usual first reaction to bad news is to think, *'What am I going to do about it?'* When I was told I had cancer I immediately had a string of questions to help me figure out a way forward. This time I had nothing. The doctor went through my other options—egg donors, adoption—and said I could also come back in a couple of years and maybe things would be better. Miracles do happen. But, he said, my oestrogen levels were exception-ally low and I was, in fact, peri-menopausal. He asked me if I'd been feeling hot, dry and emotional. I didn't know. I couldn't think at all. I couldn't speak. I felt like I was a totally different person or perhaps not a person at all.

Back at my ex's house, I suddenly became aware that he had been speaking continuously since we left the doctor. He was trying to comfort me but I didn't want to be comforted, I didn't want to know about the other options. It was the only time in my life that I didn't want to talk about an issue. The next day I was functioning like a normal person— moving around, eating and speaking— but it took me a long time before I was ready to talk about my infertility. I didn't tell any of my friends for about a month.

I have spent a lot of time thinking about the benefits of not having children, of which there are many, as well as the possibility of adopting. Both these had always been options, even before I found out that I couldn't have my own children, but that is not the point. The point is that I have been horribly cheated. I have had an essential part of me ripped away and it is very, very difficult to redefine my future and myself as a woman. I feel as though my lack of oestrogen makes me less attractive, as if men can instinctively tell that I am infertile and will take no notice of me as a result.

More than that is the fact that my partner in life will have to be someone who is contented not to have children with me. As for me, I will never be able to look at a baby and see my eyes, my nose or my knobbly knees. I will never have the miracle of another person growing inside me or the excitement of a baby's first kick. I don't fully understand what it means for my body, physically, to be going through menopause from the age of 22, but my mind is simultaneously frantic and empty.

I refuse to believe this has happened for a reason. It has happened because I had chemo, because I have cancer. It has stolen away the story of my life I've been constructing since childhood, but I am starting to see it has also set me free from it. I know that I will use this to rediscover what I really want from my life.

But first, I mourn.

Kate Paterson is a budding lawyer who loves pizza, wine and Indian literature.

My First Time Was A Disaster

Jenna Fury

THE FIRST TIME I tried to have sex was a failure. It felt like we were trying to put a square object into a round hole—it wasn't fitting and it wasn't fun.

Looking back, I realise that I had over-thought the whole process. Most of us are taught from puberty that we must think long and very carefully about losing our virginity. So, true to form, instead of allowing nature to have some say, I planned the experience as if organising a holiday trip.

I had spoken to my boyfriend about having sex with him: he was aware that I was still a virgin and I knew he had been quite promiscuous. First things first, I sent him off to Lifeline to make use of their free AIDS test. I then waited the obligatory three months, just in case, before I began to plan 'the event'.

In the interim, I visited an abortion clinic to get birth control. I didn't just go down to my local pharmacy and speak to the nurse—I had to go to the 'experts' in the industry and get the best of the best (which also turned into the most expensive).

We, or rather I, set a date when we would 'do' it on an afternoon when I had no extramural activities at school (I was 17 at the time). It started out okay as we touched and kissed, as we had done many times before, but when it came to the moment of penetration, it wouldn't go in. We tried a bit of pushing and prodding but it got sorer, more uncomfortable and embarrassing for both of us. Neither of us really knew what to do or what was wrong; they don't teach you that sort of thing in sex education.

Looking back, I can see I simply wasn't turned on so there was no vaginal lubrication. I was so nervous and tense about the whole thing that I think I literally clamped up. We decided to stop trying and he took me home.

We did end up trying again. This time I was 'prepared' but it was still not romantic or passionate. We rented an adult movie to put us in the mood, and I bought a large tub of Vaseline (I didn't know about KY Jelly yet). This time sex worked—it wasn't great, it wasn't even good, but the Vaseline seemed to do the trick. Managing to get it right seemed like such a victory to me that it never crossed my mind I had just had an experience that could never be repeated again, an experience I would never forget.

What I know now is that I was right in discussing STDs and contraception with my boyfriend, but planning the exact time of the event was not a good idea—it ruined the spontaneity and lost the magic. Be prepared, have contraception available, ensure you trust the person and have made the decision to sleep with him on your own (without coercion), but other than that, don't think anymore—let it happen when it happens and it will probably be a more memorable and pleasurable experience than mine.

Jenna Fury is an accountant who is now married to a man who makes her writhe in passion. Lesson learnt!

My First Pap Smear

Feminist Fatale

I FIRST HAD sex at 17. It was a summer's evening and my boyfriend and I were naked in the cool dusk of the room. We'd tried a few times before, but it was too painful for me despite being aroused by my lover. As I'd never been able to use tampons (my body just pushed them out), my vagina was simply unaccustomed to being penetrated by anything other than tentative fingers.

My boyfriend and I were addicted to each other, young and besotted lovers. We had had many first times together—including our first time being completely naked with a lover. After months together, having all sorts of sex except penetrative, we decided together that it was time. On that special day, it was too painful to last for more than a few moments for me, but I felt the immense intimacy and an edge of scalding pleasure of having him inside me.

Without a condom. Yes, despite the years of sexual education we'd both been subjected to in our school days, our first months of having sex were totally unprotected. My boyfriend never ejaculated inside me, so we were ostensibly practicing the 'withdrawal method'. We both knew that this was far from a safe option, and that we fast needed to find a better alternative.

Neither of us liked the taut, plastic-bag feel of condoms, so we knew that the next option was the pill. That meant, however, I would have to go to a gynaecologist to get a prescription, and this would entail the dreaded examination and pap smear.

Despite having accompanied my mother to the gynaecologist as a child, I had an ingrained terror of having to go myself. I had visions of lying prostrate on the surgery sheets, my feet in the stirrups and a lecherous male doctor peering at my cervix with a headlamp. I'd resolved that no strange man was going spelunking in my vagina.

However, as the weeks rolled past and yet another pregnancy scare accompanied a late period, I sat down for a heart-to-heart with my mother and told her that I needed an appointment with a woman gynaecologist. She was sympathetic and supportive, but wanted me to see her male gynaecologist, and couldn't understand why I insisted on seeing a woman. I wanted a woman doctor who would understand the sensation of period pains and yeast infections.

A close friend of mine passed on the number of a female doctor she had been to. As I could only get an appointment six weeks away, I grew more nervous as time went on. On the day of the examination, knowing that I was nervous, my friend passed a note to me in English class. Stapled to the sheet of paper was a rubber glove she'd taken from the biology lab, and a huge khoki drawing of a speculum that resembled an industrial drilling machine.

My boyfriend had reluctantly agreed to come along to the appointment and sit in the waiting room—it was only fair, I reasoned, that he spend some minutes reading magazines if I was to have my cervix swabbed by a stranger so both of us could enjoy safe sex. When the doctor called me into her surgery, he sank into a chair with a copy of Fit Pregnancy, and I stood up to face the ordeal alone.

The experience wasn't an iota as awful as I'd imagined. The doctor was kind and thorough, if a little harried. I had expected scratchy hospital-issue gowns, and was surprised by the array of floaty satin numbers to choose from. I slipped one on, and told the doctor I was ready. The doctor talked me through every part of the examination. She felt around my breasts and underarms for any unusual lumps, and then explained that she was going to use a speculum to open my vagina so that she could collect a swab of mucus from my cervix. This would then be sent to the laboratory and screened for any unusual cells or for other common infections, such as Candida (thrush).

Out came the dreaded speculum, which bore no resemblance to the instrument of torture my friend had drawn for me that afternoon. Rather, it looked like a mixture between a homeopathic massage device and a strange shoe-horn, and was made out of plastic, not metal.

The doctor asked me to relax, which was impossible, but as the speculum was lubricated, it slipped easily into my vagina and I felt the strange widening sensation as the speculum pressed against my vagina walls and opened me up. She took out a long implement that looked like a kebab stick with a bit of cotton wool at the top, which she put inside my vagina and took a sample of mucous from around my cervix. To be honest, the swab wasn't entirely painless. In order to get a good sample, the gynaecologist needed to collect mucous from the neck of the cervix. The action, however, only took a second. Then she withdrew the speculum and said that I could get dressed.

The appointment was over in twenty minutes, and I walked into the waiting room feeling like an enlightened, courageous and responsible woman.

I didn't stay with that gynaecologist for long. It took two weeks for her to phone me with the results of my pap smear, although she undertook to call me in half that time. In the intervening week, I worked myself into a panic that there had been something wrong with my result, and bombarded her secretary with calls, only to be told again and again that the doctor was extremely busy and would get back to me.

I found another gynaecologist with less demands on her time who gave me her cell number and told me to call her if a problem arose at any time. And call her I have, in emergency situations in different cities, from pregnancy scares to a panic about herpes (thankfully, the inflamed bump turned out to be an ingrown pubic hair).

I used to think it was unfair that women were compelled to undergo regular gynaecological examinations throughout their sexually active lives, whereas men were only subjected to such examinations if they contracted an infection of some kind, or if they needed a prostate check. But I've come to understand that this is part of my privileged and powerful capacity to bear and to sustain life. I believe a women's ability to nurture an infant inside her body and to feed it once she has given birth, is infinitely more amazing than men's ability to manufacture sperm.

Although it's ten years since my first boyfriend and I broke up, my partner still accompanies me to the gynaecologist. Why should I fight traffic alone on my bi-annual trips to the hospital for a pap smear when we both enjoy the benefits of my healthy vagina? Those well-thumbed copies of Fit Pregnancy await.

Feminist Fatale is an academic whose current research focuses on HIV and abortion in South Africa.

My First Time Learning To Breathe Under Water

Larissa Klazinga

MY EARLIEST MEMORIES are of sexual encounters with my father. The clearest one (other than flashes of oral sex-type feelings from before I had words) is of my father jacking off in front of my cot, with me holding onto the bars, the light coming into the room from the door behind him.

I was born in February 1973 at a clinic in Johannesburg, apparently to a student, and I was given up for adoption after my birthmother spent one night with me, at her insistence. I was given to an evangelical Christian orphanage and was there for five weeks before a couple who had been married for 16 years, with no children of their own, took me.

My adoptive mother continued to try to have a biological child of her own, despite warnings that it could kill her. I was about two and a half when my mother started haemorrhaging after another attempt at artificial insemination. Piecing together the flashes and scraps of memory, I think when she went off to hospital, that was the first time I was left alone with my father for any length of time and that was when he first had sex with me. Penetrative sex.

We spent most Christmases with my mom's brothers and their children. I played 'doctor' with my cousins—we must have been about four years old—and I was terrified Ouma would walk in and find us doing 'naughty things' to each other. I used to do rude things with the neighbours' kids, the Afrikaans kids next door, and the girl across the road, an English girl a year younger than me. I think I hurt the little girl, putting a pair of scissors into her vagina, and a thermometer.

We always broke out of the prison of the Highveld once a year for a two-week vacation at the coast, driving for eight hours in the family car, both my parents smoking the whole way. I was carsick the entire journey, vomiting every time we stopped at a petrol station. We had a Volvo, white with brown leather upholstery, the smell of which I will remember as long as I live—leather and cigarette smoke and dad-smell (Brut/fart/sweat/smoke/leather).

In Durban we stayed in a middle-of-the-range hotel, two streets from the beach. There was a derelict hotel partially in front of ours (The Grand), which housed junkies and prostitutes. I could just see the ocean around the huge Southern Sun hotel in front and I heard it at night, constant, like the cars below and the aircon unit. I read until my parents turned off the TV and fell asleep, then I opened the window and watched the junkies and the prostitutes and the waves crashing in the corner of my view.

I loved the ocean and going to the beach, swimming in the sea and building sandcastles. My father stopped coming along to the beach when I was five or six. He stayed at the hotel, sitting on the balcony drinking beer or rum and coke, watching the prostitutes across the road. My mother and I would go to the beach in the morning and in the afternoon she would ask what I wanted to do and, nine times out of ten, I wanted to go to the aquarium. It used to drive her crazy. "But we went yesterday," she would complain. It didn't matter how many times I went, as soon as I walked into the aquarium I was taken out of myself.

There was something about the quality of light filtered through water that took me out of time somehow, transported me to a liminal space, a place where anything was possible. If there was a god, this was her cathedral, this place of light and quiet and movement. I'd watch the sharks for hours. I'd watch the crabs, the starfish and the lobster. Everything in the ocean was clean. Baptised constantly, constantly new and free, constantly moving and becoming.

I used to dream of walking into the ocean and just keep going until the waves closed over me and the currents took me and I disappeared. I used to dream I could breathe underwater.

In adulthood I'd dream that I kept walking until the waves were rumbling high above my head and the kelp forest was all around me, tall as skyscrapers, reaching up to the light. I kept walking until I got to the cliff that separated the land from the deep water and I stepped off and descended into the dark. The water became colder around me and the world became dark and still and I breathed in the icy cold of the deep and was at peace. The dark was absolute. The cold was absolute. The quiet had never been disturbed. I was alone.

We moved to the mine property when I was about seven. By then I was beginning to be less 'baby fat' and more 'fatso'. I weighed 42kgs. I used to bleed too, anal bleeds, and the paediatrician said my diet was wrong, I needed more fibre. I carried on bleeding for another two years, until I had to be hospitalised for rectal surgery to repair the tears. No one asked any questions. Why didn't anyone say, "My goodness, this kid has gained 15kgs in 18 months and is bleeding from her arse and fiddling with the neighbours kids, something isn't quite right here"?

My father brought a German porn movie home when I was about ten and my parents and I watched it in the lounge. I got up after a few minutes, embarrassed and afraid and left the room. My father finished watching the film. I don't remember what my mother did.

My parents' room was yellow and white—my mother still has the same headboard (with my father's ashes in it.) I would lie in bed with my dad while my mom got ready to go to town, or maybe it was for church). The light was yellow through the curtains. He was naked. I remember his hands on my inner thighs, my arse, under my sleep shirt with the smiley face, no panties. "Never sleep with panties, your cookie needs to breathe," my mother said. I think she must have known—how could she not have?

I don't remember the sex clearly, though I'm trying to. I know I was lonely.

I was obsessed with videos about women being raped and exacting bloody revenge on their rapists. My parents didn't seem to mind me watching them, even though I was only about 11. I was fixated with a movie called *Savage Streets*, a terrible B-grade movie starring Linda Blair (who I later discovered was the little girl from the Exorcist). I'd get it week after week and when my parents tried to convince me to get something else, I resisted. I must have watched it 20 or 30 times by the time I was 12.

I weighed over 80kgs at 13, doubling in size in six years. By the time I started high school, I stayed indoors a lot, watched videos, read and wished I had someone to love me. I wished I had someone who saw me and accepted me and wanted to be with me. I was so very lonely, angry and isolated—all I wanted was to find 'my people'.

Over the years, my aquarium visits in Durban became a predictable ritual. I'd watch the dolphins and the seals but I loved the sharks best of all. They were perfect creatures, killing machines with no emotions, ceaselessly moving forward in single-minded pursuit of their prey. They never slept, they never stopped moving; they were strong, beautiful and I wanted to be like them. Cold, alone and without emotion, purpose-built for something other than being my father's daughter. I watched them for hours, day after day.

Back home, I would dive to the bottom of the mine pool and pin myself under the ladder at the deep end, holding myself under the water until my lungs felt like they would explode. Then I would try to breathe in. I'd surface coughing and breathing hard and then I'd do it again. It used to drive my mother insane. I'm not sure she knew I was trying to breathe down there.

I think my mother worried I was disturbed.

My parents seldom fought. My father was a typical bully, picking on the weakling and endlessly pushing to see what the limits were. My mother never pushed back, she just buckled under, fetching and carrying and 'keeping the peace'. She slept in the same bed with him year after year, despite the fact that he never bathed. She would lie there and sometimes she would let him fuck her, though she told me she never came. Sometimes there was shit on his balls and she worried about infections, but she let him fuck her anyway.

As I got older and my mother's patience finally wore off, I was allowed to go to the Durban aquarium alone. We'd still go to the beach in the morning and in the afternoon I'd split my time between the aquarium and the movies.

I used to wake from a dream where I'm lying on the ocean floor, watching the sun move across the sky through the cathedral of kelp, quiet and alone and at peace and I'd mourn the loss of it.

I didn't cry at my father's funeral, not because I wasn't sad or upset, but because I knew that showing weakness would be a fatal mistake. I stared at his cheap coffin and wondered where he was. I didn't look at his body. I should have. I was with him in the hospital the day he died, but we left before the end. My mother was incoherent after weeks of hospital treks and I made the decision to remove his breathing tube. It's not like in the movies where people take one final, dignified breath and then gently pass on. He gasped like a fish out of water for hours, black ooze bubbling from the tracheotomy hole in his throat. I told him to go and I felt sorry for him.

My father wrote me a letter which my mother gave to me after he died. In it he said that he was proud of me for standing up to him, proud of me for being my own person. He didn't say that he was sorry. Should he have? I wonder if I shouldn't have left him on the machines, pinned there with tubes down his throat.

Now, when I go to Cape Town, I go to the aquarium and sit in front of the kelp forest, watching the light filter through the water. I love the tiny bait-balling anchovy and the rays flying through the water like sea-angels. The sea is as salty as tears, as blood. I'd like to be able to say that I have shed enough of both for him and I want to say goodbye to him, give him back to the sea now. I'm washing myself clean of him, of his hands on me, of him inside me, of the filth that I used to feel permeating myself. Everything in the sea is clean, the salt purifies. If I spend enough time in the kelp cathedral, I'll be washed clean.

I'm going to have Japanese-style kelp forest tattooed on me, from shoulder to forearm. If I can't be in the sea, sanctified, made clean and whole, then I will bring the cathedral into me. I will be the whale to his Jonah. I can't cast him out so I will swallow him whole. I will grieve on my own terms, heal, be whole and beautiful by my own design in my own time.

The word for world is ocean. I'm going under, but I'm certain this time I can breathe underwater.

When I completed the tattooed ocean sleeve on my left arm after three years, I began a journey of physical reintegration. Combined with that, I worked a difficult therapeutic process facilitated by Ann, my wonderful, unconventional therapist. I can report that years of work to rebuild my self, physically and psychologically have paid off.

I don't think about dying anymore—I've survived. After years alone and at sea, my very own life guard found me. Charlene taught me the secret of breathing underwater, allowing me to see myself through the eyes of someone who loves me—I am whole for the first time in my life.

The First Time I Confronted The Idea Of Prostitution

Claire Martens

B PUSHED ME to confront my preconceptions and what I *really* believed in when he told me he had slept with prostitutes during a time of depression. I found it difficult to face the reality of his past, even though it had nothing to do with me and everything to do with him. I could label the things he did as rebellious, dark and scarring, but that was my subjective opinion.

All I could do when he told me was keep silent. What do you say in reply to that kind of confession? Can you really be okay with it, when the reality just seems so far beyond your understanding of the matter? I had always considered myself a liberal and had a vast itinerary of 'acceptable' behaviours, even though I would not have engaged in some of the activities. Nevertheless, I always tried to understand first, before I made any kind of judgement. But after B's confession, I really struggled not to feel angry and fearful. I tried to justify it from a societal perspective. I told myself that if I faced the facts, many men, married or otherwise, had sex with prostitutes. From a liberal's perspective, these women and men had the right to engage in these actions. But how could I believe that, and not accept that someone in my life who had had sex with a prostitute?

I was angry, because I had thought B was strong, and now I believed him weak. I felt that he had sullied and dirtied himself. Just thinking of the act made me feel like I was going to throw up. I felt angry that men justify this type of behaviour all the time. I was scared because I wondered if, and when, he would do it again. Mostly, however, I was angry because I shouldn't have been thinking that way. How could I be so hypocritical? How could I feel a combination of intrigue and acceptance one minute, and the next, hate prostitutes for existing?

When B told me of this, and of other things that he had done, I had to laugh with him to save both of us from my shock and pain. I had to grow up, open my mind as wide as it could possibly go, or leave him. Knowing what I had learnt, I chose to love him instead. I could not understand why, except that maybe I felt like I needed to protect him, put an end to his masochistic actions and save him from himself. By accepting his behaviour, I, perhaps naïvely, believed that it would be a purer, truer kind of love. I never got to test my theory though: he broke up with me.

I no longer need to confront the idea of a man in my life sleeping with a prostitute, yet this has not stopped me learning something from it. What B made me see was that we can never know how we will react to something until it happens to us. We can believe something of ourselves, but when someone hurts us, we can surprise ourselves by how we react to that pain. It's easy to be objective when that pain is not happening to you.

Now that we have broken up, I realise that I still have no idea how I really feel about his behaviour, but if I look really deep within me, I can see that after he told me, I wasn't really coping. Having sex with prostitutes points to a darkness, a weakness, and I cannot respect someone who behaves like that.

Claire Martens loves dancing in the moonlight.

The First Time I Was Pregnant For A Day
Elizabeth Fletcher

OKAY, SO OBVIOUSLY it wasn't really only *one day*. I was actually three-weeks-and-a-day pregnant when I found out. The decision was an easy one for me; it simply wasn't the right time. So the day after I found out, I took steps to have a medical termination and this is how it all happened.

Tuesday: 14h15

Stood in Clicks looking at the array of pregnancy tests: went for the one in the pink Toblerone-shaped box. I had to put my mind at ease after being less than responsible with the pill on a month of travel, and then having great break-up sex with my recent ex-boyfriend on my return.

15h30

Got home and dumped shopping bags on the kitchen counter. Ripped open the packet with diagrams to the effect that 'one line = exhale, two lines = knocked up' and peed on the stick. Home phone started ringing: "Bugger!" I galloped to the lounge with my shorts and panties around my knees. "Hello?" A fax tone responded: beep, beep, beep. I glanced at the stick: one line. Then, as the liquid slowly travelled further up the little window, as inevitable as a wave claiming the beach, a second line appeared. I realised I was still holding the phone, begging the fax machine on the other end to take the second line away. "No. Please, please no." The two bold lines remained. I wasn't just me anymore.

15h32

Phoned ex-boyfriend, hyperventilating. Bellowed, "I'm fucking pregnant!" with absolutely no rom-com charm. Sat on the floor in t-shirt and panties, crying and staring at those two lines in absolute disbelief, while ex-boyfriend came rushing over from work. He was totally lovely—everything anyone in my position could have asked for. He was tender, respectful and supportive of every decision I made.

17h00

Went back and bought another two tests. All positive. Like cherries on a slot machine, "Bing! Bing! Bing! You're so freaking pregnant!" Sat looking at the three tests for ages. I kept returning to them, mesmerised. Ex-boyfriend was worried it would make me sad.

19h30

Phoned my best friend who laid it down in ecological terms: "In nature, when an animal is carrying a baby and the time is not right, the animal naturally aborts. This is your beautiful body and it's your right to choose what happens to you. Right now, what's inside you is a group of cells. You've chosen to do what's best for you. You are so brave, we are all here for you."

23h00

Couldn't sleep. It was four days to Christmas and I had no idea how long any procedure would take. Googled local clinics and decided to see my GP first thing. Lay next to ex-boyfriend and talked. He kept making me laugh by pretending to fall asleep mid-sentence.

Wednesday: 07h00

Woke up and stared at the ceiling for ages before ex-boyfriend woke up. Felt the numbness of disbelief trickle into a warm, magical feeling of wonder. I felt special. I still didn't consider having the baby but the mere fact that I could fall pregnant felt wonderful.

Got up and phoned the GP. Made an appointment first thing.

08h30

Normal GP was on leave for Christmas and so had to see the other doctor in the building. As I announced that I thought I was pregnant, she responded with, "Oh wonderful! That's such exciting news!" I clarified the situation and she gave me a list of recommended gynaecologists who 'deal with this sort of thing'. After trying most of them only to hear that they were on leave, I found a Women's Wellness GP who would see me that afternoon. First, though, I needed an ultrasound to make sure it wasn't an ectopic pregnancy.

11h00

Sat in a gown in a tiny room drinking water for an hour before my bladder was full. The ultrasound was totally like the movies: cold gel, what looked like a roll-on deodorant, a black and white screen.

13h00

Met with the new gynaecologist. She was amazing. She invited ex-boyfriend in but I decided I wanted to do it by myself. She explained everything clearly without being judgemental or condescending. I had found out so early that I could use the medical method which involved taking a series of medications to terminate the pregnancy and induce a period over two or three days. She took time to understand my emotional state, my support structures and my decision making.

15h30

Took the first medication that would detach the foetus from the lining of my womb. Procedure went off without a hitch. The doctor was in touch on the phone every day. I hardly suffered any symptoms—in fact, the family Christmas (which I went to the next day) was more painful. Ex-boyfriend sat next to me for three days while my body let go.

Afterwards

It's taken a while to process it all since then—I couldn't rush figuring it all out for myself. I'm grateful that the second doctor was so great. I only wish other girls in this situation could be treated so well.

I told my family in my own time and in my own way. Maybe that'll be another story.

Elizabeth Fletcher is a reader, writer, listener, talker.

My First Post-Divorce Sex

Anonymous

THE DAY THAT we finalised the divorce, we had a dissolution ceremony in the morning: a place to rescind our vows, make new promises to each other no longer as husband and wife, a way of separating in spirit what had been joined in spirit.

I brought a bottle of champagne, we melted down our wedding rings and we made awkward conversation. My un-bridesmaid took me off to lunch where we drank more champagne, ate really good food, then hooked up with more friends to go on the rollercoaster at Ratanga Junction. Another act to embody the symbolism of what my angel-friend had been telling me: that the journey was a rollercoaster and I needed to make sure that my hands were up all the time.

We wondered where to go to afterwards. A party, yes. A chimurenga (liberation) party, even better. This was my first night of freedom as a new single woman and there was no way in hell I was going home on my own. I wanted to know what it would be like to be with someone new after 11 years of one partner, how comfortable I could be with my body in a stranger's arms. I wanted comfort, acknowledgement and affection.

Who did I find but an old admirer at the bar, someone I had consistently turned down due to my married status? It didn't take much to convince him to come home. After he lit a candle, he meandered his way across my body. He was so skinny, my husband had been solid. His nakedness was a revelation of elegance. His penis tilted to the side and he was gentle, attentive. I was surprisingly comfortable, and realised how sensual I could be, how little emotion sex required, and how different it could be. I think I may have cried. Condoms were re-introduced into my life.

Sex—easy; sleeping—impossible. He fell asleep in my bed, and I couldn't stand him being there, so I decamped to the couch. Luckily I had an early flight to catch and I kicked him out without too much discussion about why.

I was very pleased with myself.

The writer thinks life is amazing after divorce.

My First Time Getting Rid Of The Shame Of A Woman's Sexuality

Karabo Kgoleng

MY MOTHER HAD a euphemistic way of referring to our vaginas (we're all girls, you see) that left us with a sense that there was something mysterious, powerful and, somehow, also something wrong with having one. You had to keep it clean, you were not allowed to touch it except after urinating or while bathing. You couldn't look at it or pay attention to it for too long.

Ma was raised Catholic and I also grew up in the church so I understood her attitude in a way. But shame became the emotion I felt when encountering my sexuality for the first time. Even then, I still had private moments, when I would explore this 'thing' between my legs that I couldn't, shouldn't, be proud of.

The boys—my cousins, the guys at school—they had a pride about having penises. It somehow gave them the right to throw sand in our hair, waterbomb, punch, kick and tease. They could flash us and, if that happened, we couldn't tell anyone otherwise it meant that we had somehow been asking for it. A social precursor to rape, I suppose.

So the shame continued, with the dark red stain of a leaking sanitary pad at school and the shame of my first orgasm at my hands (because masturbation would surely send me to hell). The shame of not being pleased by my lover once I was old enough to have sex, the shame of lying on a hospital bed while the midwife stitched me up after childbirth, the shame of my husband's sexual rejection of me after witnessing this 'miraculous event'.

One day, I decided that this shame wasn't mine. It is the shame of a society that treats its girls and women like shit. Women can give and receive pleasure with our vaginas, we can give new life, and we can still work, provide, and be happy. For a girl, the first time people presume to know what you're about is when they say, "It's a girl." After that, you'll have more nuanced experiences of that first time over and over again. Own your femaleness, for it is yours.

Karabo Kgoleng is a young, passionate South African who is committed to building a country in which all its inhabitants can find pleasure in learning and realize their potential. She is one of the Mail & Guardian 200 Young South Africans to take to lunch, as well as the 2009/2010 South African Literary Award winner for journalism. Catch Karabo Kgoleng weekly on Afternoon Talk and on Sundays on SAfm Literature.

The First Time I Had To Deal With Rape
Rose

I WAS **18** years old the first time I had to deal with rape. I lived in a complex and my next-door neighbour was my best friend, like an older sister really. One night, when her boyfriend dropped her at the front gate, they lingered over their goodbye and that was just enough time for three men to hijack them and take them to the local township. They gang-raped my friend and forced her boyfriend to listen to her being raped at gunpoint.

My friend disappeared into herself for a long time. I cried for weeks at the loss of her—I couldn't reach her. Seven years down the line, we are like sisters again, but we never talk about it.

I was still 18 years old the second time I had to deal with rape. A group of us from my school all went to the same university and it had an intervarsity sports tournament annually. This turned into a huge party, campus was one big jam. I was in one of the dance clubs when a school friend came up to me and said, "I can't believe it, so-and-so has just been raped."

I stood on the dance floor for a while, people elbowing past me, giving me rude stares for not getting out of the way, and then I left the club, walked home in a daze and had the longest shower I can remember ever taking. Afterwards, I lay on the floor in my towel and sobbed. Two women I had grown up with, and loved and laughed with, had been violated in ways I could not imagine. I cried because it was unfair and our innocence was being ripped from us.

I watched that friend destroy herself after she was raped. She lost all sense of self preservation and actively put herself into dangerous situations because she felt she had lost everything already. She wanted to die and didn't care about the people in her life that wanted her to live more than anything in this world. The justice system failed her—her rapists went free because of one mistake in a document.

Another friend was raped in her residence room at university; the rapist then walked the corridors of our res trying all the doors to see if they were unlocked. I slept in fear for weeks. He was given kitchen duty in the dining hall as punishment and my friend left the university because she was breaking inside.

My other friend left the country because she could no longer take the stares and comments from our community. To this day she is still referred to as the girl who was raped, as if that was the defining element of her life. People start sentences with "Oh shame, yes, how is the poor dear?" and I want to hit them because she is wonderful, sparkly and fun—anything but a rape victim any more.

I have recently moved to another country and most of my friends are North Americans. We love how safe it is here—we can walk home at 2am, drunk and laughing, in a group or alone and nothing will happen. You will get to your door, into your bed and wake up feeling less than ideal, but you will be safe. I mentioned how back home in South Africa you just can't do this, not if you have any sense of self-preservation.

My friends and our parents became afraid of telephone calls that started with crying because for a while it meant that someone had been raped. I called my mother in distress once and the first thing she asked me was if I had been raped. She lives in constant fear of this.

Every year since that first time, someone in my life has been raped. Each time I become more afraid and less trusting of men. Each time I cry less because I am less soft. I am blood-boiling angry that people I love have been injured on every level of their beings. I feel helpless and that makes me even angrier.

We live in a constant state of fear in South Africa and it is not normal. It makes us angry and suspicious, it makes us hard and scared. It is abnormal and it must change.

Rose is a dancer and friend.

My First Kiss With A Woman

Late Bloomer

As a young girl, I watched way too many romantic movies. I dreamed of being swept off my feet, of knights in shining armour, and passionate kisses. I thought that love started with a kiss, that when you kissed your soul mate for the first time, sparks would fly and you would know you were meant to be together.

My first kiss didn't live up to that dream. It was a summer's day on the playground, and Christopher and I were in the sand pit building a home for ladybugs. When it started to rain, we grabbed for the ladybugs and stowed them in the barrel hanging underneath the jungle gym. We stuck our heads in the barrel and, after a few moments of idle conversation about ladybugs, he said, "Hey, let's kiss."

It was so awkward; my mouth was closed while his was open with his tongue stabbing me in the jaw, I was horrified and pulled away. As I popped out, I was surprised by a bunch of inquisitive bystanders who cheered. So my first kiss was a disaster, but I claimed it was because we weren't meant for love and that it was just a technical rehearsal.

Years went by and I was still having technical rehearsals. I had boyfriends who I thought I loved, but there was always something missing. I didn't feel a spark, no matter how hard I tried to 'fall in love'. I spent many years single and independent, a few strays would come along, a kiss here and there, but still no lightning.

I began to realise that I had been looking in the wrong place all along; I didn't feel sparks with any of my boyfriends because I was feeling sparks for my girlfriends. I guess this had been a gradual change, because I never thought I was attracted to women until late into my university years. Looking back, though, the signs were certainly there when I was younger.

I can pinpoint the day that my heart jumped for a woman for the first time. She was a beautiful, confident woman and I couldn't take my eyes off her, nor could I bring myself to have a conversation with her. Eventually, though, we talked and we became friends.

At last I got to do my first kiss over again. It was just as I imagined it would be when my knight finally arrived. We lay side by side in the dark, the crisp morning sun only a few hours away. Her hand slid into mine, my heart pounded, my palms began to sweat and my mouth went as dry as the Namibian desert. I had never felt this before. Our heads turned towards each other and we kissed, a movie kiss. At that moment, every idea I had in my head about love was questioned. My world exploded with uncertainty—all this time I had believed I would fall in love with a man, but now I was feeling the rush of love for, god forbid, a woman!

I've been in meaningful relationships with women since that day and have been surrounded by nothing but love. Not the idealistic love I dreamed up as a girl, but a real and bonding love. I've realised that, as a girl, the idea I had of love was not about a feeling, it was about subscribing to a set of conventions.

When we talk of soul mates, it's not that there is one perfect soul out there for us, it's that we fall in love with a soul. Love is the bond we create when we see the beauty in one another's souls and, when we love, we acquire an understanding of minds and hearts and we help our souls grow.

Late Bloomer is a lover of the arts and Mother Nature.

My First Time Was Awful

Anonymous

MY FIRST TIME was awful. I was 17 and distracted. When I wasn't thinking, "Ow!", I was thinking, "I'm sure he's supposed to move slightly more to the left... should I say something?"

I was raised Catholic, you see and, because not many people in The Church were having sex, we spent an awful lot of time talking, thinking, writing, teaching, praying and generally theologising about all the biblical reasons *not* to have sex. So there I was, 17, doing *it*, and though it didn't rock my world, I remember it and I will always remember it.

Firstly, because it was my first time. As unromantic as it was (after school, in his room, which smelt like old socks and Diet Coke, with Blink 182 playing in the background, condoms to manoeuvre, rushing to get it done before his mother got home and mine arrived to fetch me) and as unimpressive as *he* was (poor boy, turns out part of the problem was that I was the wrong sex), it was *the* first time.

Secondly, those ten minutes (or was it five?) were a rebel yell. Sex stood against everything Catholic in my life, it flew in the face of everything my mother had refused to say to me about sex (except to tell me, when I got my first period, that I'd better watch out because now I could get pregnant).

Sex also stood against the memories I had hidden inside me. I remember being four years old, at pre-school, and being woken up from naptime by the man who drove our little yellow bus. He touched me, kissed my skin and told me he loved me. I don't know if it happened just once, or if I've created a composite image in my head of several instances. I've had to accept that there will be patches of my memory that will always be fuzzy. I don't know if it was just me he did this to—I remember feeling special, chosen somehow.

At 11, I consciously started paying attention to all the information about 'good' or 'bad' touches. A public service announcement sticks in my memory—it depicted a suddenly depressed, moody little girl, who eventually revealed the reason she couldn't stand the uncle she once loved. I watched that little girl, and her symptoms that played out in 60 seconds; her courage and eloquence as she told her mother, "It's Uncle John; he has been molesting me." But I didn't have the words to express what had happened to me, and so I didn't tell my mother.

But you can't just hide trauma away, it doesn't work like that. I couldn't say what had happened until I fell into a deep depression, and needed to find the words so that I literally could save my life. It ripped apart my mother, whom I'd been protecting for all those years. It fundamentally changed the way my family saw me, and the ways they loved me. It changed me, and the ways I saw and chose to love myself.

I realised at 17 that I was destined to become either hypersexual or petrified of sex, and so, in my attempts to 'fix' myself, I decided I had to have sex. It was for the all wrong reasons: I didn't love the man, the relationship wasn't deep. But I had figured that 17 was the average age at which my generation had sex, and so I did it.

That first time sucked. Not because the sex sucked—in truth, it was probably no better or worse than anyone else's first time—but because the sex was merely a part of my how-to-be-normal list, while I kept burying the pain inside me.

Then I met a man and quickly fell in love with him. Being in love with him unsettled all the methods I'd put in place to bury my pain. He opened me up and somehow I was more *me* because I was with him, like Toni Morrison said, *"[he] is a friend of my mind. [he] gather me, man. The pieces I am, [he] gather them and give them back to me in all the right order"*.[1]

Within the first two weeks of meeting, it was clear we were both falling in love. We hadn't had sex though we had discussed it, animatedly. I was going to New York for a week-long conference and we were both overcome with the despair of new lovers at the thought of being apart for (gasp!) a whole week. At a romantic lunch in a fancy

---

1   From Morrison, T. 2005. *Beloved. London: Vintage.*

restaurant in Constantia before I left I told him what had happened to me.

This was before I had even admitted it to myself fully; this was before I told anyone else. There he was, loving me. *Me*. And seeing me. How could I *not* tell him this huge part of me and the pain I'd had to carry and kept shut away?

Speaking about what happened is not the end of the journey for me but it is key. I disclose it only where the context is fitting, (I haven't told the nice security guard who works the night shift in my apartment complex, for instance).When I told a group of students my grainy memory of the actual events (and for some reason, it embarrassed me how little detail I had, like there's a part of me that's asking, in an outraged tone, "*Why* don't you know more about this thing that happened when you were only four years old?'), my hands shook, I felt lightheaded. But I told them then and so I continue to tell people now. I tell through my words, I tell through my research, I tell through the way I live my life.

My boyfriend and I didn't have sex until after the New York conference. It wasn't the hurried, harried affair I was used to; I wasn't trying to be normal in some man's arms. It was him and me, bringing ourselves—our whole, perfectly imperfect selves—into a consenting, loving, sexual relationship.

Being a survivor of sexual abuse means that my relationship with my body, and with other bodies, will always be complicated. It's taken me a long time to accept this (and I don't live this acceptance everyday), but it's helped to be—for the *real* first time—in a sexual relationship where I'm allowed to bring this complexity into bed. And for the first time, I'm having great sex!

The writer is happy to report that all her subsequent times have topped the first time, and she will be married to her best friend as of December 2012.

My First Memory
Of Being Aroused
Pixie

MY TEN-YEAR-OLD SON was watching an episode of *Oprah* with me when the topic of drug addiction came up. A young rehabilitated ex-actor mentioned how being molested as a child had sent him into a downward spiral. "What's molested?" my son asked. I said, "It's when someone touches you where they shouldn't." He asked, "You mean like being raped?"

I had to explain the difference, but something else grabbed his attention and the conversation ended there. In that moment, I realized how innocent my son was. While around the world kids not much older than him were having sex, this boy had grown up so safe and so sheltered that he didn't know what molested meant.

On the one hand it's a blessing that he's so unaware of his sexuality, still so naïve and so childlike. On the other hand, it's a huge problem—he still has so much to learn about this often terrible, but sometimes wonderful world we live in. In the near future we'll have to have family discussions about AIDS, condoms, sex, pregnancy…and I wonder: shouldn't I have talked about these things with him much earlier?

When I was 11, I played Strip Poker with a bunch of girls and got threatened with expulsion when we got caught. It was the first year I kissed someone. During break, my friends and I giggled about the different kinds of condoms we had bought. Not one of us had ever had to use one, but no one would admit that, and we boasted about our imaginary sexual exploits. It was around then that I started thinking I might be more interested in girls than in boys. I was a far cry from this little ten-year-old boy who played outside on his bike around the house most of the day.

Being sexually abused awakens sexual feelings in children at a far younger age than they would have developed naturally. I remember when I was six, my granny catching me lying face down on the carpet, pressing and rubbing my fully clothed pubic bone on the carpet, searching for that warm, tingly sensation between my legs.

However, my earliest memory of feeling aroused takes me back to being about five and my last memory of being brought close to climax by the same family member is of when I was around 12. The bastard never made me come, but he himself ejaculated many, many times. How very unfair.

Feeling violated, degraded, and damaged fits having been raped aggressively or assaulted violently. But what if the abuser, the incest instigator, is gentle and loving and his hands warm and soft, his penetration smooth, although too big and too hard? What if the child's body responds with feelings of wanting more?

I went looking for more. When the abuse ended, I went into withdrawal and started having sexual encounters with as many guys as possible. I was in Standard 7 (age 15) and the guys ranged from my age to being in their early twenties. I never had full penetrative sex with any of them—I was always shit-scared—but I allowed, no, I initiated everything else. Without any exceptions, I walked away feeling relieved at not being raped, but frustrated at still wanting more. That only ever changed when I became involved with a woman.

I have a twisted sense of humour when it comes to sex. I don't think I can be blamed, I have good reason to be twisted. But do I have good reason to be gay? Is my being abused as a child and my being a gay adult directly related? This is one of many questions I've been asked, and have asked myself, over the years and the answers are never the same twice in a row.

The point I'd like to make here is that being sexually abused, assaulted or raped, whether violently or gently, always leaves the victim filled with self-doubt. Let's tell our children about the possible danger lurking in the hands and pants of every other person. Remember: the evil-doers are not always strangers or adults or men or poor or rich. They're just always on the prowl.

Pixie sings, writes and daydreams.

The First Time I Tried To Have A Baby

Anonymous

Two and a half years ago, my husband and I started trying to have a baby. (I wonder if there are a thousand and one other stories on infertility blogs that start with this sort of line?) At the time I was 27 and I was scared. Being a human being is bizarre in that way—our bodies are highly-evolved cell management systems, but we seem to have no idea what it means to produce new life. Why do we want to have babies? Should we be trying to have babies when the world has so many people in it already? Rather than having my own baby, shouldn't I rather be adopting an existing baby and helping that person to make a successful life for themselves? Are these questions even relevant? Aaargh!

After nine months of trying, obsessing and of leaving a plastic trail of negative pregnancy tests in waste-paper baskets around the house, I went to the gynaecologist. At the time, my greatest concern was that the she would scold me for planning to have a baby without visiting her first. She didn't. She suggested that my husband go for a test to make sure that there wasn't a problem with him, adding I shouldn't be concerned. The sperm test, on the other hand, suggested the opposite—the test results showed a zero sperm count.

The news closed off a piece of our future. Most of us limit our own futures, but we seldom have a part of our futures taken from us. It was a very painful experience and to try to restore things, we went into panic mode. We immediately found a fertility doctor, who started me on artificial insemination. The fertility treatments were embarrassing, invasive and it was hard to accept that the process of conceiving a baby was now a public process. After three tries at fertility treatment, I gave up.

During this period, I also went through an identity crisis, changing my job and rethinking my life plan. I began to listen to my feelings more, and to take myself more seriously.

Following my time off work, I started trying fertility treatment again. It's different the second time because I've found a way to adapt the process to ensure that it suits me: as a result, I feel much less like a victim. Not being able to have a baby has become a test in managing my feelings and maintaining hope, because if I can't manage them, I end up feeling extremely angry and resentful. I imagine walking into the fertility doctor's office and telling him that I hate him, that he's wasting my money and potentially giving me cancer with the hormone drugs.

I don't believe that we are 'meant' to go through things. I don't think that there is some higher power that is testing our characters and trying to make us better people. I do think, however, that with each painful thing that happens to us, we get the rare opportunity to look more deeply at ourselves and at life. I believe that this is, in its own way, a gift. I continue to focus on this. I look forward to having a baby to love and take care of.

The writer is on a journey.

The First Time Someone Else Gave Me An Orgasm

Lauren Cole

I'VE NEVER REALLY been comfortable with the concept of sex. Of course, that doesn't mean I've not had it. My first real kiss was at 14, my second at 17. In both cases, the guys groped me without much skill, which made me feel strange but I'm not going to lie and say some of it didn't feel good. These experiences weren't about me, they were about guys trying to score with a girl. They were short lived relationships for me.

I've always felt that sex should be intimate and beautiful. It should happen at a time when both parties are ready and they really feel something for each other. All I used to feel was lonely when I ended up in the arms of guys who merely wanted me because they didn't want to be virgins anymore. Fortunately, I was independent enough to have stood my ground and say no as soon as I got uncomfortable. The furthest either of them got was still on top of my clothes. I never touched them back.

My third kiss, though…that was something else. Just shy of 18, I was out with a guy whom I had approached and discovered liked me. We flirted shyly for a while and then, in the park, below the stars, he leaned over and kissed me. Fireworks literally went off, as there were people celebrating somewhere in the neighbourhood. I smiled and my body tingled, but I didn't let him see my fear that this would just be another guy trying to take advantage of me. Instead, we kept talking, cuddling, kissing a little more, and we kept it innocent.

I was ecstatic to find a guy who was not just using me for my body. I might have been getting As in all my classes, but my Ds were what really got the other guys' attention and I couldn't stand it. In this case, though, my new guy genuinely liked me for me. The flow of conversation never seemed to stop between us.

Like any teenagers, we didn't just talk, but we did a decent job of keeping things slow. We started out by massaging one another's backs while kissing, then progressed to kissing around the neck. Eventually, I allowed him to touch me in ways that drove me wild. Simply having his hands under my shirt, even if they were still only on my back, was a huge step for me.

The most intimate experience occurred in my house late on a Saturday night. He and I had watched a movie with my mom and her boyfriend and then they went upstairs to give us privacy. Not really in the mood for another movie, I turned on some music. We lay on the couch and talked for a bit, but soon we were kissing. He kept his hands to my lower back and hips, knowing that was what I was comfortable with. With being so close and him on top of me, we started to move together. It was at a relatively slow pace and we were still just kissing, but I ended up having an orgasm. I had masturbated (many times) and brought myself over the edge that way, but this was the first time someone had managed to make me feel that kind of pleasure, even though we were both still wearing our jeans! Right after it happened, we looked at each other, he brushed my hair out of my face and said, "So beautiful." I smiled and settled into his arms.

I'm still a virgin and I'm still with him. We haven't got much further physically than that experience, but being with him is intimate and beautiful. I can see myself with him long term and losing my virginity to him because I may be young, but I've never been happier. He makes me feel safe, never pushes me beyond what I'm comfortable with, and he cares for me on an emotional and intellectual level. I enjoy being with him in every single way, because I know I'm not just some girl to him.

Lauren Cole is a Christian teen who craves knowledge.

The First Time I Had An Abortion

Anonymous

THE FIRST TIME I had an abortion, I was 16 years old.

I was two months pregnant and had lost my virginity just two months before. The guy was the one, I had thought. I loved him to bits and thought he loved me too. But I was just a foolish kid who didn't even know how old the boy was. Looking back on it now, he was probably 22 or so.

I remember that I knew I was pregnant without even having to take a pregnancy test. I told the father of my baby that I was pregnant, but he didn't seem to take much notice of the fact. I don't know whether he didn't believed me or didn't care. Perhaps his motto was 'ignorance is bliss'.

It was a Saturday morning when I made the appointment at the clinic. On the Monday when I was going to school, I called and told the father that I was going to terminate the pregnancy. He gave a weak one-line protest, saying, "Don't you kill my child." I hung up the phone.

On the Tuesday morning I woke up, put on my school uniform and went to the hospital. My mother thought I had gone to school. When I got to the hospital, I had to fill out all kinds of consent forms for the abortion. The nurses were anything but sweet. One nurse in the administrative department shouted at me for having an abortion in my school uniform. She asked me if school uniforms were the new overalls.

It was a long day; I got there at eight in the morning and left at three in the afternoon with four pills. The instructions were to push two pills into my vagina at 4pm and the other two six hours later.

When I got home, I did as I was told. At about five in the morning, blood started gushing out of me, as though a tap had been opened in my vagina. I felt like something was sitting at the opening of my vagina and, when I went to the bathroom, I felt a soft lump pop out. The weight of the world lifted off of my shoulders.

They made me wait in a small room when I went to the hospital again later that morning. After what felt like forever, they called me into an adjacent room where I was instructed to lie on a bed with my legs stretched out. What happened next makes me cringe just thinking about it, but at least the nurses performing the procedure were really caring. I was sent into another room for an injection and then to sleep and recover.

When I woke up, I went to get medication and was ready to go. One of the nurses said to me, "Now you can have your beautiful figure again."

Looking back on the whole experience now, I am saddened by recalling it, but I give credit to the young me for having the courage to make that decision. As for the father of the baby? I've never heard from him since that Monday morning phone call.

The First Time Someone Tried To Pressure Me Into Having Sex

Jen Wynne

I WAS IN my second year at university and had had far too much to drink at a party one night.

There was a guy there that night who I really liked, but he could not have been less interested in me. A friend of his, on the other hand, took a liking to me and although I didn't like him that much I went along with it—maybe to try to make his friend jealous, maybe just to be with someone—I'm not sure which. When it came time to leave, he asked me if I wanted to go home with him and I said yes, a huge failure in judgment on my behalf. Someone offered us a lift. I thought he lived close to campus, but by the time I realized how far he actually lived, it was too late to change my mind and turn back.

Everything was okay at first, we kissed in his room, one thing led to another (it sounds ridiculous, I know)and, before I knew it, I was standing in only my underwear. This kind of thing had happened to me before, and it had always been harmless; we'd kiss for a while and then fall asleep to wake up the next day feeling awkward but fine.

I realised quickly that this was not what this guy had in mind. He was physically much stronger than me, and when I tried to push him away I got nowhere. The next ·few minutes were a blur, but somehow I managed to get some distance between him and myself, rushed to pick up my clothes and bolted out of the door, throwing on my jeans and shirt as I went.

The walk back to campus was about 40 minutes long and I cried all the way, shocked at what had just happened and angry with myself for allowing myself to get into that situation. In my head, I played out the different ways that the night could have turned out—if I had been more drunk, if he hadn't been quite so drunk, if I had given in to the pressure.

One of the things that scared me about the experience was that neither one of us discussed what was happening. We purely relied on behaviour and signals and these could so easily be misunderstood. To this day, if I am considering going home with someone, I will always pull him aside and explain that in no uncertain terms will I be having sex with him that night. Just saying it out loud takes away any possibility of miscommunication and eases everything. I haven't had a problem with a guy since then.

I know there are a ill-meaning men out there, but I think that, for the most part, we are all just people, nervous of the same things and by honestly stating what you are not or are happy to do, makes everything easier—no unfulfilled expectations, no awkward moments and no unnecessary pressure.

Sex and relationships between men and women are complicated enough, so why do so many of us continue to fuel the angst by not talking about these things?

Jen Wynne is a South African, a woman, a partner, a sister, a daughter and a friend.

The First Time
Something Embarrassing
Happened During Sex

Anonymous

IT WAS *MORTIFYING*.

We were each other's firsts, and spent many a missed lecture frantically exploring one another's bodies as though they would suddenly disappear. It was a daily activity, we were unstoppable. Everything was new, everything was exciting. Except this: this was mortifying.

That day, we tried out several new positions and so there was much, well, in and out. When I was bending over, about to roll beneath him, something unexpected and entirely new happened. Somehow, air went in and what came out was an inordinately loud fanny fart.

I immediately rolled over and, to my horror, he was laughing as though his stomach would burst. Let me just tell you there was no more oxytocin in the room that evening. I was so embarrassed I began stammering, mumbling, saying anything that came into my head, all the time thinking: *how will I survive this?* I couldn't take his laughing, so kicked him out, flung myself on my bed and sobbed.

Why hadn't any of the women's magazines told me about this? How was I to know to expect it? I was completely shocked and couldn't believe that it had happened. I was afraid it would happen again and I wouldn't know how to stop it.

When I calmed down and talked about it with him, we realised that all that inning and outing had pushed air up inside me. With the bum-lifting and squeezing, I'd been sucking it inside me. When the pressure was off, the air came out of me like it does out of a balloon with an open end.

After many more years' practice at different positions, I've learned to recognise the feeling of air inside me and now push it out voluntarily. At least now I'm less surprised! The fanny farts are still embarrassing, but I guess that's the price you pay for having good sex.

The author is still too mortified to give her name, but she still loves having sex, fanny farts or not.

The First Time I Was Touched

Anonymous

I WAS EIGHT years old when someone first touched me in a sexual way.

When someone touched me without my permission.

Since then no one touches me unless I let them—I'm 27 this year.

And even when it happens, I'm still not sure I want them to.

The writer hopes that this story gives someone hope. She says, "My past no longer defines me, I do not let it hold me back. I go through the world unharmed and only slightly altered."

My First Abusive Relationship

Scarlet Begonia

I SAW YOU again today. I felt the weight of you pressing down upon my chest as I watched your hands coming at me again and again. There was no memory of pain, just the weight heavy on my chest.

It's never full recollection, just glimpses through the haze of my subconscious. You are always there, hidden just below the surface of the person others know as 'S'. So deeply submerged and relegated to a past. A past me, a past you. A time past.

There is strangely no emotion with the memory. Just the weight: so heavy on my chest. No fear either, just suspended disbelief as I limply accepted the assault. So dreamlike in its state, through the mists of psychotropics, that at times I question its authenticity. Is this memory or empathetic fantasy—the eternal stereotype of the battered and oppressed? Am I she?

"Is this what you want?" you shouted over and over as your slaps rained down in a monsoon of emotion. I heard the reply forming in the deep recesses of broken me. Yes. Let it come to this. Beat me. Hate me. Love me. Oh, please love me, I beg of you. Feel any great emotion so that I may remain real. At least you are here, kicking me where I lie. Yes, let it come to this. From here we can sink no further and as such we are free. Yes, this is what I want. Your love. Your hate. Your violence. You above all else. I am nothing without you, as you yourself say.

We were young. Still are. I adored you from the first. So handsome and smart and damaged. You waited for me, so eager and humble and damaged. Both too desperate to be loved, and too quick to loath. I was never enough. You were always too much. The relationship was a constant give and take. I gave and you took. I slowly disappeared into you and became the part of yourself you hated the most. And I loved it. All my self-destruction manifested as a demon I could adore.

Adore you I did. I nurtured you, my beloved demon. Fed you with my nightmares, scars and insecurities. You became fat on the scraps of my self-respect, rewarding me always with the promise of love and acceptance. I gave and gave until all you had left to love and blame was that empty husk lying un-crying in the weak light of the dying day. Is this what you wanted?

"Is this what you want?" Your words slip back beyond the surface as I come up and return to the present. Such a brief moment in time I think, as you lift your weight off my chest.

I never told you how I hated the flower you bought me months after it was 'all over'. So hungry for my air, so eager to burn me up. Did you forget that once the air is gone, the fire will die too? Am I your demon? I knowingly shudder at the thought.

I shudder at all the thoughts. I shudder at the thought of your desperate death wish. I shudder at the thought of my shameful weakness. I shudder at the thought of all those who knew and chose not to say. Just another unspoken incident in a world abuzz with silence and severed tongues. I shudder for the memories always rippling just below the surface, quietly waiting to spout forth in an explosion of emotion.

Scarlet Begonia—semantic blockage.

My First Time Was Complicated
Mary-Jane Redmond

IN HIGH SCHOOL I fell in love with a guy four years older than me. My parents allowed it, but they were always worried that he would pressure me into having sex when I wasn't ready and that I would fall pregnant. I remember once my mom calling me to her room and giving me the speech about being careful, that she didn't want me to ruin my life while I was still so young. When I told her she didn't have anything to worry about, she didn't believe me. I think she may have started to when I flatly told her that unless I can fall pregnant by wind pollination, it wasn't going to happen.

You see, my boyfriend was Catholic and wasn't sure yet if he believed in sex before marriage. He had huge internal struggles with his own beliefs. I, on the other hand, while having no religious convictions about it, just didn't feel ready yet. After finishing school I went away to university and we carried on our relationship long distance, all the while remaining virgins. We went out for three years, a year and a half of which was long distance, and we broke up as virgins.

Half way through my second year of university I met 'B'. He was beautiful—tall, ruggedly handsome, and he had one blue eye and one green eye. We had a wonderful two week romance—we always knew it would only ever be that, but I didn't think he would be my first. But he was. He didn't pressure me into it, he knew I was a virgin and he was happy for it to stay that way. Our first time, my first time, was all my idea. He was gentle, we were comfortable together and while it wasn't earth-shattering, it was perfect for my first time. I didn't feel scared; I didn't feel like I was doing something wrong—it felt like it was my time.

After our first time, there were many times during our short romance. We couldn't get enough of each other and he left to go back home with the promise to keep in touch so that we could see each other whenever he came back into town. I had his cellphone number and he had my email address. While I didn't expect anything more to happen between us, I was naïve enough to think he would keep in touch. He was special to me, and I thought I had been special to him. For two weeks I didn't hear from him. When I did eventually hear from him, he told me we couldn't stay in touch. It would ruin everything for him. 'Everything?' I asked.

Yes—everything. He had a girlfriend back home that he had 'forgotten' to mention to me. He told me he was unhappy with her but that he couldn't leave her. 'Why?' I asked. Because then he would lose his son. Yes, his son— who he had also 'forgotten' to tell me about. I had used his wallet while we were together, and he didn't have one baby picture on him. Did he just not carry any, or did he take them out before letting me use it? All of this news came as such a shock to me. My beautiful memories of my holiday romance: my first time, his one green eye and one blue eye—all of it seemed tainted. I don't really know what I expected from him, but it certainly wasn't that. I guess that's what you get when you try to stretch out a holiday romance.

I'm sounding like a bitter hag, and I was for a long time. I felt used, and that he had knowingly taken my virginity from me and then betrayed me. But, while I still think he is a pig—more for what he did to his family than to me—I have tried to remember just those special memories and not what happened after.

Everyone only gets one 'first time', and he can ruin my memories of that if I let him. I only want to remember how he romanced me, how he made me feel beautiful and special, and how he gave me a first time that had been worth waiting for.

Mary-Jane Redmond is a digital marketer in the travel industry.

My First Visit To The Gynae

Swimming Fan

WHEN I WAS younger I was a really strong swimmer. I used to spend all day, and as much of the night as my parents would allow, swimming and practising my strokes. When I was eleven, I took off my costume one day and I noticed that inside my vagina was a small white lump. It looked like a blister or a pimple. I touched it and it wasn't sore, but I got scared. What was this lump? What was it doing in *my* vagina? Was it supposed to be there? Did *everyone* have this lump and I was just late in getting mine?

So after much looking at this thing and wondering about what it was (remember that this was before the days of Googling every lump and bump on your body), I went and asked my mum. Mum had a look, and said she wasn't sure; we had better go to a doctor.

Her gynaecologist was a man, I was terrified. The door to his room was white, and the curtains were that light turquoise that I've now come to associate with hospitals and medicine. When I sat down on the bed, I had to take off my panties and I wasn't sure where to put them. Should I leave them on the floor? Should I hold onto them? I didn't really want to give them to my mum, as that would be weird. So I just held them in my hand, lay back and thought of swimming. He asked me to open my legs.

He had a look. I waited, wondering if I would ever recover from this fear. That was the most my vagina had been looked at in its life. He turned to my mum, and said "It's just a little cyst, nothing serious. It should go away by itself."

"By itself!" I screamed in my head. I had come all the way here, opened my legs and shown my vagina to a stranger to tell me that it would have gone away by itself. I blushed crazily and was very happy to unravel my undies and pull them on faster than I've ever done since then. We left and my mum tried to placate me by saying every woman had to go to the gynaecologist, and that I shouldn't be embarrassed. I remember gazing out the car window, determinedly not looking at her.

When I got home, I realised that it wasn't that scary. After that day though, I'd never again choose a male gynaecologist. If I want a man to look at my vagina, it's going to be when I want him to—not for medicinal purposes.

So I went back to swimming, and thought that it was an entirely suitable activity until that time came.

Swimming fan still hates going to the gynae regardless of how this particular incident ended.

The First Time I Told My Mother About My Sexual Assault

Anonymous

WHEN IT HAPPENED, I didn't think much of it. I was drunk and we kissed, and then it was more and I said no, and asked him to stop, and I cried, and he held me down with his knees and forced his penis into my mouth.

The next day, I saw him and he didn't even look at me. I've never seen him again, and I don't think he'd recognise me if he did.

He was a year or two younger than me, and dating a friend of a friend. I hadn't known he'd had a girlfriend, and I felt guilty. When I woke up the next morning, I vomited and blamed myself. I felt guilty for years. I put the incident down to stupidity, regretted it and then thought I had got over it.

When I was twenty-two, though, I started thinking about it. I realised that it had affected me more than I knew. I spoke to friends about it, went to a therapist, and eventually, when I felt like I was dealing with it, I told my mother.

She said she thought I was overreacting, that people make mistakes, that it would be better if I just forgot about it.

Part of me knew she was right and that it could have been so much worse. But all I'd wanted was a hug.

We've never spoken about it again.

The writer is a feminist student who loves coffee.

The First Time I Didn't Want To Put My Hand In The Air

Lindy Mtongana

IT HAPPENED IN a makeshift theatre that had been rigged up in a large classroom of a local high school. There were close to 200 of us, tightly packed in, sitting side by side on those rickety steel grandstands—the kind where the complimentary cushion provides little comfort and does even less to prevent your backside from going numb.

The actors had just finished a performance of *The Vagina Monologues*. There was generous applause from the audience, pleased with itself for engaging with this groundbreaking and controversial piece of feminist theatre. In truth, though, I suspected none of us were quite sure what to feel. We had laughed, we had recognised ourselves in some of the characters portrayed, and we would talk about the play when we made our way back onto the bustling streets of the National Arts Festival. But few of us really knew what the appropriate emotional response was to a series of stories about women and their vaginas.

When one of the actors signalled for us to quieten down, the applause faded and, in a voice that projected across the classroom, the performer said, "Would those of you who are willing, please raise your hand if you have ever been a victim of sexual abuse or assault of any kind."

At least four of the six actors were the first to raise their hands. The audience was less eager to divulge. The question had taken us by surprise and obviously it was deeply personal. Even so, a few people in the audience tentatively rose their hands.

Then the booming voice filled the room again: "Would those of you who are willing, please raise your hand if you *know* someone who has ever been a victim of sexual abuse or assault of any kind?"

This time, without much hesitation, hands shot up in the air throughout the room. We all knew someone. No doubt, some of those who were too shy earlier were raising their hands for themselves as victims.

I thought of those I knew. A friend who was molested as a child. Another who was sexually abused by an uncle for close to a decade. Another who was raped in her first year of university. And a classmate who, after becoming a drug addict and nearly losing her mind, was informed by her parents that she had been raped at the age of two by an uncle. They had withheld this information from her, hoping that the memories and the trauma would never resurface.

Suddenly I felt as though my heart was cracking open, like a dam wall breaking before the water comes rushing through; I could feel the first stirrings of the emotional response the play and the ensuing exercise elicited in me.

Looking at the room of raised hands, my feelings flowed out in confused and contradictory bursts. First anger at the violence that has been meted out to women across this country. Then gratitude for the fact that I need not count myself as one of its victims. Then shock that I should *need* to be grateful to have never been a victim of sexual violence.

The chilling reality stared me in the face—that the sexuality of women in South Africa was, and continues to be, severely compromised by how pervasive sexual abuse is in our society. I think that what should be a God-given right for any woman, the right to their own sexuality and sexual pleasure, comes down to luck in the end. I was lucky to own my vagina. Unlike many women in South Africa, my sexuality was mine to enjoy and experiment with. The journey of my sexual discovery would not be tainted by memories of violation, fear and pain. My vagina was mine.

I wished all women could say the same.

I left the theatre that night with a prayer in my heart, that a generation of South African women free from abuse was close at hand. I pleaded with the heavens that if a booming theatrical voice should ever address those questions to an audience again, not a single hand would be in the air.

Lindy Mtongana studied Journalism and Drama at Rhodes University. Over the past five years she has worked as a journalist in online media and broadcast. She currently works as a news anchor for eNews Africa, a division of the eNews Channel.

The First Time I Fell in Love With A Girl

Nadia Barnard

THE RELATIONSHIP WAS like a shooting star, it shone brightly but faded quickly and it happened so fast, I was still digesting the idea of us before it was all over.

I was working as a manager at a restaurant when she started working as a waiter, fresh from the UK, living her life as fully as she could as a full blown lesbian. I instantly found her attractive but ignored it. To be honest, I've always been attracted to both men and women, a bit of a bi-curious streak. When she was also made a manager, we had to interact more. I tried to keep our relationship as professional as possible, but it seemed impossible. Before I knew it, she was joining my friends and me when we went out.

Things started to get more intense, especially at work. My attraction to her started to consume my every thought. It got to the point where I could barely be in her presence without dropping something, walking into something, or uttering incoherent ramblings. I felt like an idiot. My mind kept screaming at me: "Step away from the girl, I repeat, step away from the girl!" I also knew she was going back to the UK soon, but like a moth to a flame, I couldn't resist her. She realised it and began to pursue me.

She invited herself over to my house for dinner; there was enough nervous energy between us to blow the roof of the house. When it became late, my housemate suggested she spend the night and I hastily retreated to my room while she stayed behind on the sleeper couch. My heart was racing, a million and one things running through my mind. I was unable to think straight, unable to sleep. I knew I was at a crossroads.

So I chose one of the roads and texted her, asking her to come to my room. We sat on the bed for a few minutes—a mini eternity—and then started kissing. Before I knew it, I lost my virginity for the second time, this time to a beautiful girl. There were no real firework moments—the best was afterwards, lying cuddling and being in the moment together. We stayed awake most of the night talking and exploring.

The sleepovers went on for about a month. No one at work knew and that added fuel to the excitement of the experience. There were glances, words, subtle touches. I tried to convince myself the relationship was just for fun. But each sleepover wasn't just about the sex; it was also the emotional and intellectual connection we shared, getting to know each other better. When the dreadful goodbye was upon us, with only one week left before she went back to the UK, I realised I wasn't just falling in love, I was crushing in love.

A few days before she left, she came to my house after goodbye drinks for her at work. She confessed that she slept with one of the other managers, a guy, and it had happened at work the previous weekend. Suddenly the whole fairytale crashed into a million pieces. Her excuse was that her dad didn't want her to be gay, so she gave it one final shot with a guy. She told me she loved me and it made me furious. How can you break someone's heart like that and then tell them you love them? It is like deliberately punching someone in the stomach, then saying sorry and expecting that person to accept your apology.

We talked before she left; I wanted to fix the unfixable. I kept saying it wasn't her fault I was so upset, that it was my own because I should have never allowed myself to fall in love. All the alarms and smoke signals had been there. I blamed it on the movies, on fairytales, for making us believe that nothing can stand in the way if you love someone.

I felt desolate about the whole experience for months after she left. I was depressed and couldn't believe that someone who knew how you felt could make you feel so miserable. One of my friends once told me, don't screw the screw. If only I had listened.

Nadia Barnard is someone who loves new adventures and ticking items off her bucket list.

The First Time I Was Nervous About Sex
Anonymous

I GET NERVOUS about sex. In fact, I've always been nervous about sex. I'm not sure why. I was never abused, never pressured into something I didn't want to do, never had the 'fear of God' put into me.

I never really discussed sex with anyone when I was younger. I think I was given a couple of books, but never had 'the birds and the bees talk'. I don't know why, because my parents are liberal and we aren't religious. In fact, when my boyfriend came to stay, it was me, not them, who thought it better that he stay in the spare bedroom.

I first had sex when I was 20, in a bathroom stall on the platform of a tube station in London. We weren't dating at the time, but had been previously and I wanted to 'get it over and done with.' It wasn't very romantic, and I was drunk, but at least I loved the guy. To be 100% honest, I'm not even sure if we really 'did it' because there was no blood at all. I'm pretty sure there should have been blood.

Fast forward a couple of years and the second 'first' time I had sex was with my long-term boyfriend. Again, I was drunk and I suspect I did it to remove any doubt of him going back to his 'fuck buddy' for want of a better word. There wasn't any blood on the sheets either, but after I got up the following morning, there was a sudden whoosh and my pants were drenched. I freaked out, but felt I didn't know the guy well enough at the time to talk to him about it. I raced to the bathroom and then spoke to my digs mate who calmed me down.

Sex with that boy was alright. I probably can count the number of 'great' times on one hand. We broke up after two years, but I lost interest in having sex with him after a year and a half, probably because I realised we were never going to be long-term (I was leaving the university town and he was staying). Sex became uncomfortable. I began to dread it and thought of as a chore. That's not great when you're supposed to be in your prime and wanting to rip one another's clothes off!

Since then, I've not had sex. Oh, I've thought about it, on many an occasion. But I'm scared. I'm scared it's going to continue to be uncomfortable for me, that I'm going to forget what to do, that it'll be a fuck up and I'll never enjoy it.

My doctor assures me not. She says I'm probably tense because, on top of being nervous, I'm now worried it's going to be uncomfortable. In fact, she advocates that when I am in a long term, healthy relationship again, I should lock myself up with this new man for extended periods of time to 'get used to sex'!

I want to enjoy sex—I'm desperate to, in fact—but I'm worried about letting myself go. I'm thinking of buying myself a 'toy' to get used to my body again—perhaps then

I won't be so closed off and nervous and altogether just plain scared.

The writer is a believer in romance.

My First Encounter With Semen

Anonymous

I WAS EIGHT when I first encountered semen. I was also eight when I saw a fully grown hard-on pulsating penis; it looked like a dark, writhing monster with a swollen red head, the colour of an open wound.

I never saw that penis much, because the boy was always pressing down on my pelvis and legs, and my head was almost always looking up at the ceiling. If my head wasn't looking up, it was looking to the side, checking the door in case someone walked in on the shameful act. He was 17 or 18, his beard was already sprouting and his penis was huge. I knew it was large before I even saw it because when we all had to sleep in the same room, he would press it up against my bum, or make me touch it under the blankets.

No one questioned the wisdom of putting an adolescent boy in the same room as young girls. It was partly our black way of thinking—all the children are our children, they share everything and the older ones take care of the younger ones. During the day, the older one would find ways to sneak me into a bedroom when the adults were gone and hump me fully clothed. His sister was two or three years younger than him and I think she knew what he was doing, but chose not to walk in on it.

I'm convinced she knew because, on the night of the semen story, she was sleeping on the bed and we were on the floor. The television was on; we were watching a late-night film, and we hadn't switched off the lights. It bothered me that the lights in our room were on because I knew what was coming and was afraid the adults would come in and catch us.

The boy was sleeping in our room again because an activist was on the run from South Africa and his room was the only one available for that man. He always set it up that I ended up next to him and that night it had been, "Let's stay up and watch films, why don't you get off the bed so you don't disturb my sister when she wants to sleep?" I always obliged, so I got on to the floor and we watched the television from his temporary sleeping area.

When the moment seemed right, with his sister snoring on the bed, he rolled up on top of me like he normally did. This time, he escalated things. He unzipped his pants and, although I can't remember exactly what he did in the seconds that followed, I remember the panic that came over me because I was afraid we would get caught. But what I feared the most was that he would actually put his penis inside and have sex with me.

On the floor, on my eight-year old back, I looked up to his eyes, hoping he would read my anxiety, but he was unrelenting. I whispered "Please don't do that. I'm going to fall pregnant." He whispered back, "No, don't worry, that only happens to grown girls like my sister." *No, no you don't know that it can also happen to me!* I wanted to plead reason because I had read in the paper a story about an eight year old who had fallen pregnant. I didn't want to wake anyone, so I quietly said "No, no Sbu, no." I tried to keep my legs tightly together.

We battled with my underwear for a few seconds. He won and threw my panties under the bed; I watched where they went so I could find them afterwards. I don't know what happened after that because I can only remember the light on the ceiling, the worries in my head, his weight. I was ready for anything.

But very suddenly, he rolled off me, onto his side and made a grunting noise.

I sat up quickly and saw a whitish blob on the carpet. He went to the bathroom, leaving the damning evidence behind. I hoped he would return quickly to wipe it away, we always had to remove traces of these acts. I did my part by looking under the bed, but it was dark and I couldn't find my underwear. Careful not to wake his sister, I got into bed, hoping it would be easier to spot my entangled panties in the morning light.

The next morning, when I woke up, I saw that the white blob had disappeared and I was just very relieved.

The First Time I Wanted To Be Pregnant

Anonymous

THE FIRST TIME I took a pregnancy test, I was shitting myself. I was a twenty-year-old student and had been in a relationship for less than a year. As my parents were strong Christians, they believed that sex outside of marriage was a sin. In other words, if that pregnancy test had popped up with a little plus sign or a goddamn smiley face, I would have been in a really difficult position. Thankfully, it was negative.

The second time I took a pregnancy test was earlier this year. I had just come back from a glorious honeymoon in Egypt, my period was late and my tummy playing up. I waited and waited for my period to come, but no show, so I took a pregnancy test. This time was so different to that first time I peed on a stick. This time, although I was on contraception and hadn't planned to get pregnant, I was half-hoping that those two positive lines would show up. It wouldn't be ideal—we were newly married, not financially stable yet and barely able to look after ourselves and our little flat, never mind another human being. Yet...

Truth is I *wanted* to be pregnant. I wanted to feel my breasts swell and feel the stirring of new life deep within me. I wanted the ultrasounds and late night cravings. Okay, so I don't really want the nausea, the haemorrhoids or the earth-shattering (pelvis-shattering?) pain of childbirth. But I wanted the child, the baby at the end of it all.

But then again, I also wanted to be able to drop everything and go away for a surprise weekend with my husband. I wanted to be able to go out and get crazy tipsy with my friends, to sleep through the night and lie in on weekends until noon if I wanted to. I wanted to have the odd naughty cigarette when I was stressed or on a night out, for my body to remain within my control and my lady bits to stay the way they were. I wanted my marriage to remain about us as a couple, and not just us as parents.

So, now I'm torn. Half of me is obsessed with having a baby, and as each birthday ticks by, the more appealing it becomes, which I'm sure can partially be blamed on hormones and my biological clock ticking. The other half of me, however, doesn't want to become a mama—not just yet. This half is worried about the practical and financial implications, never mind what being pregnant would do to my body, my social life and my relationship.

For now, I am still relying on the marvels of modern contraceptives and enjoying living a selfish, child-less life. But, if that second pregnancy test had turned out to be positive, it wouldn't have been such a disaster after all…

The writer likes good books, chocolate and fruity white wine, preferably at the same time.

The First Time I Gave Away My Virginity

Anonymous

I WAS 16, 17? I don't remember. What I do remember is that my mother had spoken to me about making my first time special. Making sure I loved who I would be having sex with, making it memorable with use of the usual romantic props—flowers, candles, perhaps trying to prepare me for the fact that sex the first time wouldn't be great, so why not use the props to have something nice to remember.

I may not remember the age, but what I do remember is that somehow I had convinced or hoodwinked my mother in order to be at a club with my friends. I remember that I always got a rush out of being admired, even more out of being hit on.

And there was this sailor. Sweet man. I don't know how much discernment I practiced, I don't think much. I think that I was so flattered by the fact that someone liked *me*, that I would have taken whatever came my way. So we hooked up, I don't remember how. We must have been kissing in the car park, he had such a hard on.

And then he used all those old lines that I knew were bullshit to talk me into sex. His balls would turn blue, he would be damaged, how could I lead him on like this? So what did I do? I gave in. We made our way to the highly romantic toilet stall. My flowers were the khoki-painted walls covered in graffiti. My candles, the sullen overhead fluorescent light of the toilet stall. I lost my virginity to a sailor in a toilet stall in a club at 17.

I didn't think much of myself or the occasion then, and now all I have is compassion for my younger self, yearning so much for affection and love, with all her mild rebellion, with her 'I don't really care' attitude who gave herself away so early, and from then on, so consistently…

The First Time I Knew I Wasn't Ready For Sex

Anonymous

I WAS IN my first year of university, naïve and passionate, when I had my first real boyfriend. The word 'boy' in boyfriend is significant, as he truly was just a boy.

We met in a crowded nightclub, and had our first intoxicated kisses, which were repeated on the many drunken nights in the same place. Shortly, we became boyfriend and girlfriend and began our lustful, rocky relationship. Between the sheets of his single residence bed, as we listened to the slow beat of Bryan Adams CD over and over, we explored each other's bodies. He told me he loved me and I reciprocated, as far as I could understand about love at the time. My face glowed with delight at his romantic attentions, so much so that others often commented on the change. I remember thinking that if everyone else thought we were in love, then I must be.

Over one of the holidays, I travelled the long bus trip to spend a week at his house. I was slightly shocked on my arrival to find out that his parents allowed me to stay in his room and share his double bed. During those heated summer nights, we became increasingly experimental in the bedroom. We had never spoken about sex, though, and so he frustratingly fought against invisible boundaries that I had set up inside my head but never voiced.

I was a virgin, unsure how far I was comfortable or willing to go. He was sexually confident and eager, but never knew, or thought to ask, how I felt about sex and my virginity. I did know, though, that I was not going to give myself completely to him, but I had no idea how to break this news to him.

On my final night at his house, exhausted from late night after late night of the same pattern of refusal, I fell asleep in the middle of one of our make-out sessions. Unaware of the impact of this on the male ego, I was stunned by his response when he stormed out of the room. He returned a bit later with a storm on his face to tell me that we had become like an old married couple. He climbed back into bed, turned away from me and went to sleep.

We had to travel on the bus together the next day, and the trip remains in my mind as one of the worst days of my life. He ignored me the whole eight-hour trip home, only bothering to reply when I asked him a question. Every now and then I looked at him closely and asked if he was ok, or reached out to touch him.

When we finally reached our destination we said goodbye, and after two days of silence he phoned to break up with me. I sobbed uselessly on the phone, confused by the reasons he gave. I was completely heartbroken.

Only years later I came to understand why exactly he broke up with me, and I know it is because I wouldn't sleep with him. Looking back, however, I don't regret dating this first 'boy' and I'm glad that I kept myself for someone who was willing to wait.

The invaluable lesson I learned from this first relationship is the importance of communication, especially with regard to sexual boundaries and personal values and standards.

The writer is a primary school teacher who is happily engaged and believes in the power of love to overcome all obstacles.

My First Time Was Not My First Time
Francesca

FOR AS LONG as I can recall, I've never been a virgin. In my teen years, when my peers were proud of their virginity, I hoped that no one would ask me whether I was still virgin. I'm not sure if I would have been honest. I remember being grateful that it was not part of my culture to be tested for virginity because I would have had to explain myself and disgrace my family. So I hid my virginity status and, since I'm an introvert, most people assumed I was one.

The question came up with my boyfriend years later, though, and I couldn't run away from it this time. He got me to the point one evening where my mind and body were begging him to enter me. Unlike the other times, I let him go all the way. Suddenly he was huge on top of me, heavy; I disconnected. I opened my eyes and looked at him, no longer feeling the pleasure of the thrust, gentle as he was, but instead the terror of being pressed down. Moans of pleasure turned into winces of pain and panic.

There was something painfully familiar with this picture. Me vulnerable. Him powerful. Me the victim, he the perpetrator. He was my unknowing rapist. He was enjoying a moment that brought me pain, fear, vulnerability and hatred. I willed him to stop, my mind screamed, but my mouth did not cooperate. Here I was again, helpless, pressed down, small. The object of this man's pleasure.

He must have felt the disconnection, because he stopped and pulled away slightly. I took a deep quivering breath. At the moment he was that perpetrator and I hated him. He looked at me. "Are you okay?" he asked and hugged me tightly. I cried in his arms, realising our special moment had been haunted. He asked much later in our lives, "When we made love for the first time, was it your first time?" I responded, "Voluntarily, yes..." My first time, and second, and third, and fourth...were in fact at the age of five with a sixteen-year-old uncle.

I'm not fond of sharing stories about my first time, as it was anything but special and loving. Every day is yet another struggle to lock it away into the deepest part of my unconscious mind.

Francesca (not her real name) is a researcher and humanist who believes in the inherent goodness of people.

The First Time I Bought A Vibrator
Dorothy Black

IT SEEMED LIKE a good idea at the time. We were drunk and I'd
been talking about it for a few months, threatening to just
go ahead and do it. I was also a little tired of my girlfriends'
jaws dropping every time I said I'd never tried it before.

There was a group of us. Safety in numbers. There's a
first time for everything, right? It wasn't far to go, though
as I stumbled down the street to that place, you'd think I
might have reconsidered and chosen a more sober-minded
moment to go ahead with this.

But we'd gotten the guys in on the idea, and they were
even more excited than us. It's not that I wasn't okay with
the idea, it was just so personal and now I had an audience,
people would see what I was into. It started freaking me
out a bit. But suddenly we were there, my friends were
giggling and awash of beer-fuelled bravado pushed us
through the entrance.

Adult World. That bastion of cheap 'n nasty, a wank
warehouse. My friends grabbed my hand, pulling me to
The Great Wall of Dildos—an expanse of candy-coloured
plastic and jelly creations, with glittering rubber vulvas
and B-grade porn stars gasping and pouting from cheap

cardboard inserts. There my friends left me to find 'The One' (it's so personal, after all).

I'd just broken up with my boyfriend and, not having any other starting point, scanned the wall looking for something that vaguely resembled his proud member. Thin and long, no. Veiny and blue, no. Bubbled and curling with lights, um...nope. Then, suddenly, in a burst of luminous pink jelly, I found my ex's plastic penile doppleganger. I took it out the packaging, fitted my hand around it and measured it for girth. I almost put it in my mouth.

My friends, back again from squealing over gaping anuses and poking fake tits, gathered around me, sizing up my choice. They found it good. We went to the counter, where a helpful, unwashed old man showed me how to insert the batteries, working his palm up and down the shaft without taking his eyes off me. Had I not been sufficiently liquored up, I probably would've wanted to vomit.

But I had just bought my first vibe with an audience and had not gone cheap, baby. I'd spent almost R200 on this buzzing fucker and was thumbing my nose at my ex's member in the process. I was practically invincible and nothing could scare my vagina. Also, there's nothing a little boiling water and soap can't fix. I named it Percival and it was good.

Dorothy Black is a sex journalist and supporter of sex-positive thinking. Like most South Africans, Dot enjoyed a religious, sexually fraught and emotionally uneducated upbringing, and stumbled into sex and adult relationships in much the same way we all do—badly. After much experience, therapy and opinionating, Dot did what every self-respecting egoist does: Write about it. And here we are.

The First Time I Had A Miscarriage

Anonymous

THE FIRST TIME I started writing this, I gave a blow-by-blow account of the events of my miscarriage. While it may have given a picture, it didn't convey the emotional pain of it. Now a month later, having read the account, I can see it as a stage of the process of dealing with loss. Getting to grips with what happened, running through the series of events to figure it out, make sense of something that as far as I'm concerned shouldn't have happened, and still shouldn't be.

I'm left with loss, anger and great disappointment. It was a risky pregnancy from the beginning—disconcordant twins—but despite the risk we dared to dream. We spent hours imagining our new lives as parents of twins. Debating names, thinking of the next steps, getting our excited heads around the very wanted, happy expansion of our love and family.

Then something went wrong and for two days, we shuffled from a doctor without ultrasound, to a doctor with ultrasound, to gynaecologist with even better ultrasound. She confirmed that one of the twins had already gone, and that the other had no heartbeat. I was referred to a person whom my medical aid would pay for to do a D&C (where they scrape out your womb).

With varying levels of compassion, and with various bedside manners from people who helped us, we sunk into a cycle of hope and despair. It culminated in tears rolling down my cheeks as I sunk into the unconscious state of the general anaesthetic, probably the most alone and out of control I've ever felt in my life.

Waking up after the operation, my first concern was what happened to the tissue that would have become my babies. When I asked what did they did with it, the nurse replied immediately, comfortingly, that the tissue would be burned—not a proper burial, or any ceremony to mark my loss of dreams—but burned, so at least it wasn't sitting in a bin somewhere, thrown away like a piece of rubbish. For some reason the distinction was, and still is, very important to me.

Then we had to start telling the people who had known about the pregnancy that we were no longer pregnant. It was a responsibility I abdicated, especially in the first couple of days. I didn't want to speak to anyone, or have to deal with any sympathy when I knew sympathy was all most people had to offer. I didn't want to have to talk about it to anyone. Most people have no idea of the extent to which the miscarriage still impacts on me, mostly because I won't show, and I won't tell.

Then when I did start talking, I got hit by an overwhelming response of people's stories of their own loss of children, early miscarriages, stillborns, horrific experiences with doctors and medical staff, of the lack of choice, and many of their subsequent pregnancies.

What I'm left with is a sense that, like rape or domestic violence, miscarriage is so common in women's lives, yet they keep silent. Women are at the mercy of doctors and other professionals who are vague about the impact of miscarriage. In my case, I wasn't even told there were alternatives to a D&C operation (like waiting for the miscarriage to bleed out naturally, or taking medication to push the bleeding along).

Like a friend who shared her rage with me that, when she chose the option of medication that would initiate cramping and bleeding, her doctor told her she would experience routine cramping and pain, and fairly heavy bleeding. It turned out she had blood-splattering, earth-shattering pain that required medical attention. Like the other friend whose doctor gave induction drugs until the baby was killed. The caesar that followed resulted in stillbirth and then, to add insult to injury, she was stitched up so badly that she became infected and had to go back three times.

The doctors give vague information about allowing yourself time to mourn, and being aware of the impact of shifting hormones and a re-adjusting body. The mood swings, the overwhelming irritation that could make something as simple as a cutting a tomato the wrong way turn into an end-of-the-world event and result in crying. The vividness of nightmares and the shame of loss.

There is the silence, the veil of 'secrecy' that exists about how common this occurrence is, that the figures of between one in four, and up to 40% of pregnancies are known miscarriages (some never know, just have a heavy period). Until you start telling your story and you find out how common your experience is. And the thing that sucks—that makes absolutely no difference! In fact, it makes me feel like I need to deal with my grief that much more quickly, to learn to cope because other people do, all the time. While I don't want to define myself by my loss, I don't want it to congeal into a major part of my identity and because of this, I'm struggling to allow myself room to feel, room to mourn, room to be angry that life has not turned out the way I thought it would. Guess I'm still learning that lesson in every way.

The writer is a fully recovered and expecting mother.

My First Guilt-Free Masturbation

Anonymous

I MUST HAVE been 13 years old when masturbation first occurred to me. I was sent an email of cartoon characters performing various sexual acts and one of them was Princess Jasmine, her hand moving back and forth on her vagina, looking vaguely bored. Up to that point, my sexual experience had included only a hand mirror and me after an interesting guidance lesson in Grade 7. I couldn't fathom how this strange mess of flaps and folds could give me any pleasure.

In the years that followed, wanting to know what sex felt like without actually having sex, I poked and prodded and am embarrassed to say I even used the back of a hairbrush once in the hopes of knowing what all the fuss was about. (The hygiene-freak I have become is queasy at the thought.)

By 15, I started dating, and sexual exploration became something naughty. My vagina and I got disconnected— it wasn't something for me and my enjoyment, but something I could use to get boys to like me. After a while, though, I learned that boys liking my vagina was actually very different to them liking *me* and I started to respect my body and myself more.

I fell in love with a boy when I was 18 and had sex for the first time. We had a lot of sex: excellent, good, average, and ugly. Sometimes I loved it and sometimes I hated it, but I felt like it was something we had to do.

My friends and I spoke about sex quite thoroughly, but masturbation was never mentioned. The only time the topic was ever raised was when men brought it up in a drinking game, like Truth and Dare. My friends always vehemently denied that they did it. "Yuck!" they said, and they still do. I think it's something to do with the word 'masturbation'. It conjures up images of dirty sex shops or shady men wanking in their car in public places. It's for perverts and 12-year-old boys.

It was only recently, some years later, that I gave masturbation serious consideration. Having been single for a number of months, I was beginning to get frustrated, dreaming about sex almost every night and waking up pining for a man to put me out of my misery. I was still reluctant to masturbate—it was masculine, dirty and I probably wouldn't be able to do it right anyway. Luckily, I came across an article in a magazine about orgasms being good for your health, and one morning after a particularly vivid dream, I decided to give it a go.

I wasn't sure where to start having sex with myself—I closed the curtains and took off my clothes, but then thought surely some kind of ceremony was required. Should I light candles? Should I bath first? I got back into bed and concentrated on reviving the dream I'd been having as I tried to work out the mechanics of the clitoris. When there was no immediate sensation and I couldn't even remember the dream, I almost gave up.

But I was determined not to fail. Soon I was fully aroused and I realised that a little bit of light rubbing can go a long way. I couldn't believe how easy it was; it was the most natural thing in the world and I didn't feel dirty at all. In fact, I felt totally liberated. I now see it as a way of looking after myself, like healthy eating and exercise.

It is so empowering to know that the thing that makes me sexy is me, not how I look or what I wear, and certainly not because a man thinks that I am.

The writer loves daisies, chocolate and taking herself for long walks on the beach.

The First Time
I Ejaculated
Anonymous

FEMALE EJACULATION: I KNEW it existed. I had read about it, even seen it on some dodgy late night sex show. None of this prepared me for it happening to *me*. I was freaked out. I was grossed out. Inspecting the 'wet patch', I was reassured that I hadn't just peed myself—the liquid was clear and odourless. I was still freaked out. My partner was in awe of it—I think he found it fascinating and exotic.

To me, ejaculating feels completely different from a 'standard' orgasm (is there such a thing?). Whilst the latter is a hard, pulsing sensation, the former is more of a physical release—a warm giving-in to pleasure and of what your body is demanding of you. I prefer a normal orgasm, it's more earth-shattering.

Is this purely because I'm not used to ejaculating yet? I've only 'squirted' a handful of times and it still shocks me. Researching the matter hasn't really helped. There has been little research done on the subject and there are a myriad of different theories, descriptions and causes. Some claim it never happens, other dispute when it happens—during orgasm or before. Most of the information out there seems to be based on anecdotal testimony.

Indeed, considering how much research has been done and how well understood male ejaculation is, it's shocking (but perhaps not surprising) that so little is known about the female version—especially in the highly sexed world we live in. Perhaps if more were known about it and it was talked about more, women like me wouldn't be so freaked out when it happens.

Back to my experiences of it: I am completely in awe of my body's ability to do such a thing, even though I don't fully understand why and how. I think that I have some way to go before I can embrace it and enjoy it thoroughly. Thankfully I have a lifetime of sexual escapades ahead of me to find out!

The writer likes good books, chocolate and fruity white wine, preferably at the same time.

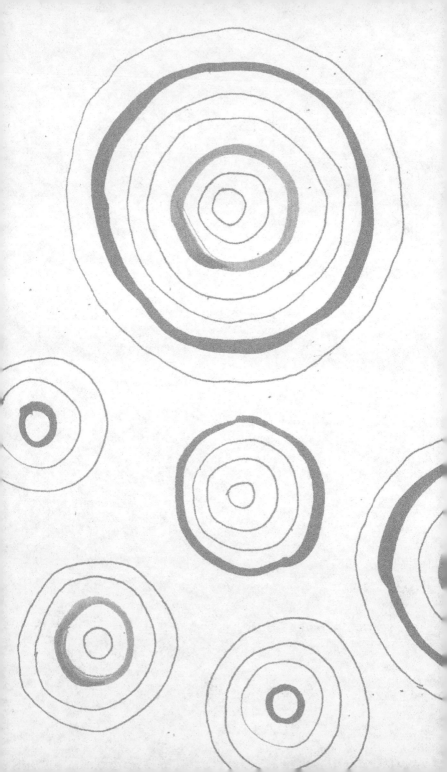

Join Us

I would love you join the *My First Time* project too. There are many ways that you can do this.

You can read this volume of powerful writing and then share it with a sister, a mother, an aunt or a friend. Perhaps this will give you the courage to share your story.

You can visit the site http://myfirsttimesa.com and comment on the stories online so that you give support and affirmation to the women who shared them.

You may find that a story you read here sparks something in you, or rekindles a desire to share one of your first times. If you do have this feeling, then I encourage you to write what you feel and write honestly. I am always glad to receive them and to share your story online.

If you would like to write a story for the project, please send an email to 1sttimewritingproject2010@gmail.com.

I want women to feel like they have a safe and powerful space to be themselves, to share their stories of joy or sadness and, importantly, to know that on the worst day they've had so far, someone else knows how they feel and would love to comfort them.

This project and this collection of stories is here for you. Use it as you need to.

Love,

Jen

Acknowledgements

IT'S HARD FOR me to think of a time before *My First Time* was alive and real in my life.

I want to take the opportunity to thank my boyfriend, Mike Baillie, who believed in me throughout, who helped me build and design the blog, and who has always been so proud of this project. I learnt how to make a blog from him and I think that, with his initial help, I've actually gotten quite good. Cubes, Scoobs.

Thanks to my family of courageous women. I found my roots with you, and you are always so supportive of my growth. It means the world to me.

Thank you to Carla Kreuser for the cover design and to Nella Freund for the editing. Thank you to Colleen Higgs from Modjadji Books who gave us all the opportunity to grow and learn from one another's stories, and who supports Southern African women writers.

I cannot thank the writers enough for sharing stories with me and now with you. Some were my friends, who amazed me by coming to the party with some of the best writing around. Others were complete strangers. These women took a chance in emailing me their most personal and private stories, and all they had to go by was a tiny 'about me' section. I thank them for coming on this journey with me, and I hope that their bravery will inspire you to get writing and sharing, either with us online, or with each other in real life.

NARRATIVE NON-FICTION TITLES BY MODJAJI

Invisible Earthquake:
A Women's Journal Through Stillbirth
by Malika Ndlovu

Undisciplined Heart
by Jane Katjavivi

Reclaiming the L-word:
Sappho's Daughters Out in Africa
edited by Alleyn Diesel

Hemispheres: Inside a stroke
by Karen Lazar

http://modjaji.book.co.za